LEARNING FOR LIFE & WORK

EMPLOYABILITY

FOR CCEA GCSE

COLOURPOINT
EDUCATIONAL

Paula McCullough

© Paula McCullough and Colourpoint Books 2011

ISBN: 978 1 906578 72 5

First Edition
Second Impression

Layout and design: April Sky Design, Newtownards
Printed by: W&G Baird Ltd, Antrim

COLOURPOINT EDUCATIONAL

Colourpoint Educational
An imprint of Colourpoint Creative Ltd
Colourpoint House
Jubilee Business Park
Jubilee Road
Newtownards
County Down
Northern Ireland
BT23 4YH

Tel: 028 9182 6339
Fax: 028 9182 1900
E-mail: info@colourpoint.co.uk
Web site: www.colourpoint.co.uk

The Author

Paula McCullough has over 23 years experience of teaching in Northern Ireland and examining at GCSE, AS and A2 Level. She is currently head of the Religious Education Department at Methodist College Belfast and also teaches LLW to GCSE level.

Acknowledgements

Once again, it has been a pleasure to work with Rachel Irwin, Editor at Colourpoint. I am indebted to Rachel for considerable advice and support. I would also like to thank Colourpoint Books for giving me the opportunity to work on this whole series for LLW.

A few other people helped with the text or offered advice. I would particularly like to mention Mary McSorley of the Equality Commission Northern Ireland for her help with employment legislation. I am also very grateful to the business people who contributed their experiences of self-employment. Jill Armer at CCEA has offered valuable advice throughout the whole series. Many thanks!

This writing project has been made easier by the support of my family. This book is dedicated to my husband Frazer and sons Peter and Michael.

CONTENTS

Chapter one

THE IMPACT OF GLOBALISATION ON EMPLOYMENT

CHAPTER SUMMARY

In this chapter you will be studying:

- **What is meant by 'Globalisation'.**
- **The impact of global economic changes on Northern Ireland.**
- **Changing employment patterns.**
- **Migration and immigration.**
- **The growth of new technologies.**

THE GLOBAL ECONOMY

Think of all the products you might wear, use, eat or drink in a typical day. It is quite likely that a number of these will have been produced in Northern Ireland, perhaps your bottled drink or bread for your lunch. However, take a look at the labels on your clothes and you will see that most of these have a different country of origin, along with many of the electrical and electronic items you use. This sourcing of products from different parts of the world shows the economy operating on different levels – locally, nationally and globally.

> **Info Box**
>
> The **economy** of a particular country, or area, is concerned with:
> - The production of goods and services.
> - How these goods and services are distributed and consumed.
>
> This will involve a consideration of the resources that are available, such as land and workers, and the demand for a product.

Many people think it is important to support local farmers by buying goods that have been produced in Northern Ireland. Why buy vegetables that have been flown halfway around the world, when choosing local produce helps create job opportunities and is better for the environment? Local farm shops selling home grown vegetables and meat are becoming increasingly popular. Many of the large supermarkets make a point of selling fresh produce that has been sourced in Northern Ireland, as well as goods from other parts of the UK and overseas.

MCGEES BUTCHERS – A LOCAL FARMSHOP

Our fourth generation farm at Gortnagarn in the highlands of Co Tyrone has a proud heritage as a fine heard of mixed grass fed cattle including native breeds such as Angus and Hereford. These breeds provide superior meat and do not require routine medication.

People complain about the weather in Tyrone, but it's the soft mizzly rain that gives the grass and our meat their sweetness. There is no need for chemical fertilisers which force growth in the pasture and the beef. This slow easy pace is absolutely crucial to the distinctive taste and texture of our meat.

We pride ourselves on our high standards. These are achieved by constantly assessing and reassessing every aspect of our business. We do this by constantly listening to our customers and staff and by keeping abreast of new developments within our industry.
Having our own farm and our own shops in which to sell our own beef allows us to give our customers that essential element of trust that every customer requires when they purchase meat today.

McGees in partnership with ASDA

McGee's Butchers has gone into partnership with the supermarket chain in a deal which could create at least 100 new jobs across Northern Ireland.

"This is a positive and progressive move for the local retail sector offering a prime NI butchery business the opportunity to grow alongside the province's most popular supermarket," said John Deasy, NI Manager of ASDA.

"We've listened to our customers and know that locally sourced food is a priority, but value, quality and excellent service are also so important to them – and this is exactly what we're offering through our partnership with McGee's. It also further highlights ASDA's support for the NI agri-food sector – from farm-gate to checkout."

Joe McGee of McGee's Butchers added: "This is a great concept, bringing together the best of both worlds by combining supermarket shopping with local expertise. It should be regarded as an important investment in the age-old craft of butchery, offering customers the level of service, experience and advice which they often seek, but which is becoming increasingly hard to find in today's fast moving retail market."

Information taken from http://www.mcgeesfood.com/main.htm

ACTIVITY

*Read the case study on **McGees Butchers** and **ASDA supermarket**.*

Discuss your answers to the following questions in pairs, then produce your own written answers for your folder.

- In what ways is McGees a good example of a local business?
- What traditional methods does McGees farm rely on?
- Using information in this article, what do consumers in Northern Ireland want?
- How will this partnership between McGees and ASDA attempt to meet the needs of customers?
- How will this partnership benefit the jobs market in Northern Ireland?
- How can a national supermarket chain and a local business help each other?

We also like to have a variety of goods available to buy that cannot be produced locally, perhaps because of climate. Oranges and bananas need to be imported from countries with sunnier climates, for example Spain or South America. Cost is another consideration, as people want to buy goods at the most competitive price. In some parts of the world, such as India or Korea, people are prepared to work for lower wages. It may be therefore cheaper to import items such as clothes or electronic goods than to produce them locally.

In the past, there were limited opportunities to buy and sell overseas. Nowadays, fast and efficient transport systems and electronic communications make world-wide trade part of our everyday lives. This is all part of a process known as globalisation. It can bring enormous benefits to our lives, but there are also disadvantages in terms of impact on the local economy and possible unemployment for the people living here.

WHAT IS 'GLOBALISATION'?

If something is described as 'global' then it involves the entire earth, not just a particular country or region. 'Global' therefore means 'worldwide'. The issues of climate change or greenhouse gases, for example, are global concerns as they impact the whole planet.

Globalisation is the process of the world becoming more interconnected and interdependent.
People around the world are more connected to each other than ever before, largely due to advances in information technology. You can chat online to friends who are thousands of miles away, while businesses can move money and secure deals at the click of a mouse. International travel is more frequent and

available to more people than ever before. Countries also rely on each other much more than in the past and depend on other nations for:

- resource trade, such as food, oil or raw materials
- disaster relief, as in the recent cases of the earthquake in Haiti or the floods in Bangladesh
- support (from allies) in times of war

Globalisation is also seen in trade and business. Goods and services produced in one part of the world are becoming increasingly available in other parts of the world. Through globalisation, the move is made from local and national economies to a global economy. Globalisation connects people across national, geographic and cultural boundaries.

DISCUSSION

"Globalisation is creating a shrinking world."

- What do you think this means?
- Do you agree or disagree?
- Can you think of any examples?

IMPORTS AND EXPORTS

As a result of globalisation, most countries in the world, even those considered to be less well developed, export their own produce and rely on imported goods from overseas.

Imports refer to the products, services or raw materials which are brought into a country. A country's **exports** are the goods and produce which are sold abroad.

Northern Ireland imports and exports a wide range of goods, services and products. Some of our exports include meat, dairy and bakery products; ready meals and convenience foods; laboratory equipment; quarrying machines and generators; computer software and medicines. Imports into Northern Ireland cover an even wider range of produce, from computers to confectionery, and vehicles to vegetables. Some imports to Northern Ireland are in the form of raw materials to be manufactured locally, while others are the finished product that has been made overseas.

RESEARCH ACTIVITY

Using the Internet, find as many different examples of imports to Northern Ireland as you can.

What would your life be like without these items?

CASE STUDY: NORBROOK LABORATORIES LTD

Norbrook Laboratories Ltd produce medical, veterinary and pharmaceutical bulk material, based in Newry, County Down.

"Since its foundation in 1968, Norbrook Laboratories Ltd has grown to be one of the world's leading pharmaceutical companies. With manufacturing facilities on four continents and sales and marketing offices in over 30 countries, the company exports to more than 120 countries worldwide.

Norbrook's success is a combination of a number of factors, including continued investment in research and development, a focus on global markets, innovative business techniques, first-class production facilities and an unwavering commitment to quality.

Norbrook has recently been awarded the Queen's Award for Enterprise 2011, which is given for the highest levels of excellence in recognition of the company's outstanding

continuous achievement in International Trade. It was also listed as one of Europe's Top 50 Growth Companies in 2010, an accolade which was awarded to entrepreneurial companies whose "ingenuity, hard work, perseverance and capacity for innovation have shaped a successful and growing business, significantly contributing to the creation of new employment and prosperity in Europe." They have enjoyed an annual increase in export sales of 15% year on year in the three-year period since 2007. In 2010, export sales contributed more than 90% to the Group's consolidated turnover.

The company's focus for the future will be to identify and maximise opportunities from overseas markets and to continue to invest in research and development to ensure a strong new product pipeline which will support continued global growth."

Information taken from http://www.norbrook.co.uk/index.cfm/norbrook

KEY QUESTION

What has helped to make Norbrook Laboratories a successful business with global trade?

THE IMPLICATIONS OF THE GLOBAL MARKET FOR NORTHERN IRELAND

The impact of globalisation and worldwide trading has both opportunities and potential drawbacks for Northern Ireland.

Here are some considerations:

 Northern Ireland has the opportunity to trade on an equal basis with countries all over the world. This could prove to be very beneficial for the local economy, by bringing in money from overseas buyers and leading to an increase in employment.

 Town twinning can develop opportunities for exports and joint ventures, such as investment links and projects.

Global trading can lead to an investment in advanced technology and training for businesses in Northern Ireland. This could result in a more skilled and motivated workforce.

 Firms in Northern Ireland competing on the world market might find global trading is very successful and gives their business a boost. This could have very positive results, such as an increase in trade and employment of local people.

 However, some manufacturing businesses may be unable to compete. As a result they may have to close, or be taken over by a larger firm, leading to staff redundancies.

WHAT IS TOWN TWINNING?

Town twinning is the idea of pairing cities across the world as a way of making links between nations. It first started in Europe in 1930 and became a popular practice following the Second World War, as a way of creating friendships and understanding between countries affected by the war. Town twinning quickly spread to other continents as well.

Town twinning often pairs towns and cities with similar characteristics. This pairing can lead to cultural links, economic trade and student exchanges.

Cookstown has been linked with Plerin Sur Mer in Brittany, France, since 1995. During this time there have been regular exchange visits between the two towns.

Bangor, in North Down, is twinned with Virginia Beach, USA, and Bregenz, Austria.

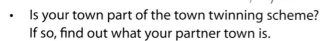

RESEARCH ACTIVITY

- Is your town part of the town twinning scheme? If so, find out what your partner town is.
- What activities have taken place recently?

WORLD-WIDE BUYING

When products are imported and exported, this can benefit the consumer, the business and the local economy.

Here are some of the advantages of buying and selling products worldwide:

 More variety – One of the main advantages of imports is that we get a much wider variety of food, clothing, electrical items and other goods. The climate in Northern Ireland is unsuitable for growing many of the items that are part of daily life. Imagine having no tea, coffee, bananas or sugar, for example! Most people would consider these imports to be a necessity. Having a greater availability of items to buy increases our standard of living.

 Competitive prices – Often goods that are imported from overseas are cheaper than locally produced ones, even when the cost of transportation is taken into consideration. Competitively priced products from abroad can encourage local producers to try and reduce their prices, which is good news for the shoppers!

 An increase in profits – A local business can make more money and therefore be more successful as the result of marketing products abroad.

 An increase in employment – A successful business will be able to expand, as increased sales lead to higher levels of production. This expansion can lead to the creation of new jobs and a reduction in unemployment. Individuals benefit from this and the local economy also gets a boost.

 Political reasons – The government often encourages businesses to market their products abroad by offering financial incentives. One of the benefits of foreign trade is that it can promote good relations with other countries throughout the world.

1. What is meant by 'globalisation'?
2. Explain the terms 'import' and 'export'. Give examples of each.
3. Write a short paragraph to explain how people in Northern Ireland can benefit from global trading.

SOME OF THE DISADVANTAGES OF GLOBALISATION

Some businesses in Northern Ireland may encounter drawbacks as a result of globalisation. Perhaps they are simply too small to operate on a world-scale and it may not be possible to compete with larger businesses. On the other hand, if they do not take advantage of overseas markets, they might find themselves being squeezed out of business altogether.

Here are some of the issues that need to be considered:

- **Will there be language barriers?** New staff may have to be recruited or existing staff trained to speak the appropriate foreign language.
- **Can my business cope with an increase in demand?** More orders and an increase in profit are one of the attractions of trading overseas. However, the business will have to be fully equipped to cope with increased demands for goods. This could mean employing extra workers or increasing the available storage space. Money will have to be spent on expansion and a small business could find themselves in financial difficulty if the increase in demand is only a temporary one.

- **How will the goods be transported?** A business will need to spend some time researching suitable transport arrangements before entering the global market. It may be that the cost of transporting the goods makes it too uneconomic for buyers overseas.
- **What currency should be used for an overseas transaction?** There may be problems with the currency used by the country wishing to trade. The impact on the prices of goods with exchange rate fluctuations will also need to be taken into account by a business thinking of trading overseas.

- **What official documentation is needed in order to trade overseas?** The business will have to be familiar with the documentation needed for trading with countries overseas. This may take time and effort – and careful consideration will have to be made about whether the extra business potential justifies this. Some countries will have government regulations in place, which will need to be carefully researched beforehand. A business will also have to consider VAT (Value Added Tax) as there are different responsibilities for this depending on whether goods are being sold within the EU (European Union) or outside the EU.
- **Is the product suitable for selling outside Northern Ireland?** When trying to sell a product overseas, it may be necessary to be aware of local customs and traditions, to make sure the product is appropriate for the people living there. It will be essential for a business to carry out market research to make sure there is a market for the product.
- **What about existing customers?** If a business is putting a lot of effort and resources into developing overseas trade, then there may be less focus on the market at home. If existing customers are lost, this could be very serious if global trading turns out to be unsuccessful.

However, despite some of the drawbacks, many developing businesses in Northern Ireland have managed to expand successfully by entering the global market. There are a number of organisations that exist to give advice to businesses about trading overseas (some of these will be studied in Chapter four). The widespread use of computers and information technology has also helped some local businesses to expand globally. The term **e-marketing** refers to the promotion of products or services using the Internet.

WHAT ARE THE ADVANTAGES OF USING THE INTERNET?

There are many ways in which a business can benefit by using the Internet to market their goods, especially if this business wants to trade overseas.

- **A global market can be reached** – Traditional ways of marketing a product, such as a newspaper advertisement or a poster on a billboard, are expensive and are usually limited to large companies. E-marketing opens up new possibilities for small businesses, on a small budget, to reach customers from all over the world.

- **There is the scope to offer a wide range of products and services** – Businesses can use the Internet to promote a variety of different services as well as simply advertise goods for sale. For example, a customer can choose a holiday destination, research available flights and book online.

- **The Internet is interactive** – Through the use of email, use of the Internet allows for conversations between a business and potential customers with queries about a product. Feedback from customers helps a business to improve its services and be more successful.

- **The Internet is immediate** – With use of the Internet, a product can be bought straightaway, so business hours are increased to 24 hours a day, seven days a week throughout the year.

- **Particular groups of customer can be targeted** – Through market research, businesses know what 'type' of person is more likely to purchase their product. E-marketing can be used to target people with specific interests, depending on the websites they use. When you visit particular websites, you may have noticed that related adverts often pop up.

A further benefit is that use of the Internet has led to the creation of many new jobs. More and more companies worldwide are recognising the business opportunities of e-marketing and are seeking to employ people with the relevant media and IT skills.

CASE STUDY: CHAIN REACTION CYCLES

Chain Reaction Cycles is an example of a business that has had great success from e-marketing. The business is based at Doagh, in Co Antrim.

Chain Reaction Cycles (CRC) was established in 1984 starting out as a small independent bike shop and since then has grown to become the world's leading online bike store.

In June of 2005 CRC moved to new purpose built premises. At the planning stages the decision was made to incorporate a state of the art showroom into the new location enabling our customers to call in and experience the personal side of CRC.

CRC ship products all over the world, with its core business comprising of bikes, parts and accessories, CRC also sell snow boarding equipment and clothing, motocross parts and a vast selection of branded sports clothing, and boys toyz. They stock many of the industries' top brands.

During its development CRC has won many awards for its website and business practices. The Managing Director, Chris Watson was also nominated for Entrepreneur of the Year 2006.

Information taken from http://www.nijobs.com/Chain-Reaction-Cycles-Ltd-Jobs-2833.aspx

DISCUSSION

Read the following examples.

Can trading on the Internet help these business people?

Do you think their business would be suitable for the national or global market?

- McLaughlin Brothers is a small market gardening firm. Brothers Patrick and Dermot grow fruit and vegetables on their farm which they sell locally to small shops. They also have a stall on a Saturday market.

- Irish Crafts specialises in handcrafted traditional items, such as Aran sweaters, bodhrans and silver jewellery. Their products are popular with tourists and the business is doing very well.

- AB Electronics is owned and run by John single-handedly. He sells electronic components, circuit boards, and parts for computers. His small outlet on an industrial estate is fairly busy, but he also does quite a lot of mail order business.

- Cakes For Fun is a side-line of a local bakery and specialises in decorated cakes for special occasions. Customers can choose from a variety of designs or have their own idea created in coloured icing.

DISCUSSION

What jobs might be created in Northern Ireland as a result of globalisation?

Assess the impact of trading on the Internet to a business.

EMPLOYMENT IN NORTHERN IRELAND

Today, there is a wide variety of different occupations and careers available. As society develops and daily life becomes more complex, the jobs that people do also change to reflect this. This is one of the reasons why careers advice is so important. There may be some areas of employment you are not even aware of!

A SHORT HISTORY OF EMPLOYMENT IN NORTHERN IRELAND

- Traditionally, the main occupations were in agriculture. Many people worked the land to produce food or were involved in processing the end product, such as milling grain or weaving cloth. Other jobs included blacksmithing or producing farm tools.

- The Industrial Revolution in the eighteenth and nineteenth centuries brought about many changes to traditional employment. The linen industry provided work for many and saw the movement of people from farming occupations in the countryside to mill work in the towns. By the beginning of the twentieth century Ulster was the most important linen centre in the world, with more than 70,000 people employed in the industry. The development of steam-powered machinery also saw radical changes in agriculture, manufacturing and transport. By the late 1800s Ulster was one of Europe's leading manufacturing regions, with Belfast home to both the largest shipyard and largest rope works in the world.

- The Second World War had a significant impact on the economy and the labour market. Many people had jobs that met the needs of wartime. Agriculture and food production remained important, and there was further growth in engineering and shipbuilding.

- Unemployment fell during the war years but by 1955 unemployment in Northern Ireland was around 8%, higher than anywhere else in the UK.

- By the 1960s, employment patterns were changing again. Less people were employed in the traditional industries, but there were opportunities brought by new investments, and Northern Ireland became the location for a number of new factories making man-made fibres. Financial help for farmers was also introduced in the form of 'deficiency payments'. This was to ensure that they received a decent payment for their produce, even if prices fell.

- The period of political unrest known as 'the Troubles' began in 1969. The violence continued until the ceasefire by most paramilitary groups in 1994, followed by the Good Friday Agreement four years later. During this time, many investors from overseas were discouraged from coming to Northern Ireland and unemployment was a serious concern.

- Since the late 1990s the situation has slowly improved as investors have gained confidence in Northern Ireland. Many new residents have recently come to live in the country, seeking job opportunities. By 2008, unemployment in Northern Ireland was lower than the rest of the UK. The retailing industry received a boost as many large UK stores decided to invest in Northern Ireland. Recent arrivals include Tesco, Sainsburys, Asda and Iceland. During this time, the IT industry started to expand and a number of investors located call centres here, bringing further employment opportunities.

- The economic downturn of 2008 brought feelings of uncertainty as once again unemployment increased and many people experienced a lower standard of living. However, Northern Ireland is slowly recovering from this period. Government forecasts suggest that over the next decade there will be an increase in demand for ICT skills, health and social care, retailing and leisure work.

ACTIVITY

Produce a timeline to show some of the important developments in employment.

WHAT ARE THE MAIN AREAS OF EMPLOYMENT TODAY?

- **Agriculture** – This has always been one of Northern Ireland's most important areas of employment. However, for many years there has been a decline in the number of people employed in agriculture. One of the reasons for this is that advances in farming technology have meant that fewer people are needed to carry out the same tasks. Although there has been a decrease in those involved in traditional farming, the number of people employed in food processing and food production has increased.

- **Manufacturing** – Some of the famous names in manufacturing over the years have been Bombardier Aerospace and Harland and Wolff. However, there are other smaller manufacturing companies which are also important employers. Glen Electric, based in Newry, is one of the largest manufacturers of home heating appliances in the world; and Retlan Manufacturing in Toomebridge is one of the leading trailer manufacturers in Europe.

- **Tourism** – Since the Good Friday agreement in 1998, Northern Ireland has moved on from 'the Troubles' and into a period of relative peace. One of the main industries to benefit from this has been tourism and hospitality, which includes the hotel trade. It is thought that tourism will be a significant growth area in the near future, as Northern Ireland becomes increasingly popular as a tourist destination. Some of the most popular tourist attractions include the cities of Belfast, Derry and Armagh, the North Coast, Giant's Causeway and Northern Ireland's many castles.

- **Retail** – This is the largest sector of employment in Northern Ireland and it is vital to our economy. Retail supports local industry and agriculture, as it is the way in which produce is sold to consumers. However, some small businesses in the retail industry are struggling to survive because of the arrival of large chain stores that they cannot compete with.

- **Construction** – This area of employment includes skilled labourers, engineers, architects and surveyors. The construction industry in Northern Ireland had steady growth until the economic downturn in 2008. This led to many job losses as the local housing market slumped and building projects were cancelled.

- **Information Technology** – In recent years, this has been one of the main areas of growth in Northern Ireland. A local workforce of skilled IT graduates has led to large amounts of investment from outside Northern Ireland, and resulted in ongoing development in this area.

IN THE FUTURE...

In general terms, the occupations people have reflect the society we live in. For example, there has been significant growth in the IT industry as computer technology is playing an increasingly important part in our lives. Other areas of employment that seem likely to expand over the next few years are the **Leisure Industry** and **Social Care.**

Occupations in leisure include those in sport, fitness, travel, entertainment and catering. Even in a time of economic downturn, people still need to enjoy leisure activities. Now we are slowly recovering from the 'credit crunch' occupations in leisure are likely to increase further.

Careers in social care typically include working with children or the elderly, in a residential setting, day centre or caring for someone in their own home. Advances in medicine and health care over recent years have meant that people are generally living longer, so there are more elderly people who need to be cared for.

Nowadays, many parents choose to continue with their careers, rather than stay at home to look after young children. Nurseries and play groups for pre-school age children are increasing in number and so are the opportunities for a career in child care.

Most people nowadays are aware that it is important to care for the environment. We are asked to reduce, reuse and recycle – and are given plenty of opportunities to do this. In fact, **recycling** is now making an important contribution to the economy.

LOCAL ECONOMY GETS BOOST FROM RECYCLING

NEWS ITEM

Recycling is emerging as a leading force in the Northern Ireland economy.

That's the message from Bryson Recycling, Northern Ireland's largest recycler as it revealed that the materials it handled for recycling directly support around 1,000 local jobs, through collection and remanufacturing, as well as many other related jobs in the service and transport sectors.

Bryson has seen significant growth in the sector over the last five years, with an increase in the amount and type of materials that can be processed within Northern Ireland contributing to its economic value. 35% of the materials handled by Bryson, amounting to 20,000 tonnes annually, are now reprocessed by companies in Northern Ireland, who turn the materials into products that fetch around £14m per year.

Eric Randall, Director of Bryson Recycling, which is part of the Bryson Charitable Group, said the industry has enjoyed remarkable growth recently.

He said: "Over recent years recycling has emerged as a leading industry in Northern Ireland, sustaining growth and creating jobs at a time when many industries have experienced a decline in demand and have had to make thousands of workers redundant".

All of the glass collected through Bryson's kerbside box collection service, for example, is processed by Glassdon in Toomebridge before going on to Quinn Glass in Fermanagh where it is used to make bottles for local brands such as Bushmills and Magners. Cherry Polymers in Antrim manufactures pipes using the plastic bottles collected, while paper is sent to Huhtamaki in Lurgan where it is used to make moulded fibre products such as egg cartons.

Source: http://www.brysonrecycling.co.uk/

ACTIVITY

Read the news item on Bryson recycling.

Prepare a one minute talk entitled 'How recycling can benefit the whole community' to present to the rest of your class.

CHANGING EMPLOYMENT PATTERNS

What is a career? For many people, their idea of a career is to start work when leaving school or university and stay at their chosen profession until they retire, perhaps with promotion or added responsibilities along the way. However, employment patterns are changing and for an increasing number of people today their career path will not be like this.

As a young person soon entering the present world of work you will probably not have the same occupation for life. You will have to be prepared to be more flexible, possibly moving to a different area to stay in work or having jobs in a number of different industries. In the future, working from home will become more common for many people, as will flexible working hours and fixed term contracts.

Here are some reasons why employment patterns are changing:

ADVANCES IN IT AND USE OF COMPUTERS

Over the past number of years, advances in information technology have led to many employment trends being based around computerisation. Many people now use the Internet for shopping, which has changed the way many retailers carry out their business. Some find it no longer economical to maintain a shop at all, as customers prefer to browse on their computer screen in the comfort of their own home. Many people would prefer to choose and book their holiday online rather than visit a travel agent. These changes mean that less people might be employed in occupations where face to face contact is needed with customers.

Almost everyone has a telephone in their home and most households now have a computer. For many occupations this reduced the need for employees to actually go into work, as their jobs can be carried out from home. This new way of working is called teleworking. For businesses there are a number of benefits to having employees working from home, as they can use their workspace differently and may be able to reduce costs, such as money spent on electricity. Many employees prefer this, too, as teleworking is very flexible, can fit in with childcare arrangements and cuts out the time and money spent commuting to and from work.

TELEWORKING

The Office for National Statistics (ONS) has defined teleworking as:

"Working in a location that is separate from a central workplace using telecommunications technologies to enable this."

Source: Labour Market Trends, October 2005,
http://www.statistics.gov.uk/downloads/theme_labour/LMT_Oct05.pdf

As well as a computer and telephone, a teleworker may also need access to a fax machine. Some teleworkers do not actually work at home but at a dedicated telecentre near to them with access to IT equipment.

HOT DESKING

This is a result of employees only needing to be in the workplace for a day or two each week as most of their work is carried out off-site. Hot desking is a situation where a desk, computer and workspace are available to anyone who needs them in the organisation, on a flexible basis.

SKILLS TAUGHT IN SCHOOLS

Many of the skills taught in schools reflect these trends in the workplace. You will have noticed that ICT is used in all subjects, as well as being taught as a separate area of learning; this is to help you have essential skills for the world of work. Whatever your chosen career you will need to be proficient in numeracy, literacy and in the use of computer technology.

THE NEED FOR RE-TRAINING

Older people who have been working for a few years may find that the skills and knowledge they acquired when training are quickly becoming out dated. This is especially true with computer skills, as technology is moving so rapidly in this area. Employees have to accept that re-training is now an important part of any career to keep up with modern technology. Some people may have to re-train and learn new skills as jobs in some of the traditional industries are being lost. There are now fewer workers in primary and secondary industries (farming or ship building, for example) but an increasing number of people in the service sector (restaurants and entertainment, for example). Some manufacturing jobs in Northern Ireland are declining as locally made produce cannot compete with cheap imports.

CHANGES IN LIFESTYLE

As previously mentioned, widespread use of computer technology in the workplace has to led to some employees **working from home**. This suits many people as they would prefer to work flexible hours, rather than the traditional 'nine to five' office hours. In the past, many women gave up their careers to bring up a family. Today this has changed and women are becoming more and more prominent in the workforce. With teleworking, a couple can arrange for one parent to be at home to look after young children.

Another lifestyle change is that more people have **part-time work**, perhaps to fit in with family arrangements or maybe because they have more than one part-time job. In recent years, we have become more of a 24 hour society, with many of the larger supermarkets and some garages open around the clock. This means that employees will need to be flexible, but also have the opportunity to work shifts that fit in with their other commitments. Different employees will have different needs, for example, a parent might prefer to work during the day when the children are at school, but a student would be available for evening work.

Short-term contracts are another feature of this more flexible attitude to work. An employer may use a short-term contract if they think the work might be temporary and are unwilling to commit to a permanent contract. An example of this might be seasonal work, such as retailing work leading up to Christmas. An employer may use a short-term contract to employ someone to carry out a particular task, such as a research project. Short-term contracts give flexibility to the employer but for the employee there can be uncertainty over the future. However, some employees welcome the opportunity to do a range of different tasks, building up their skills and experience.

COMPANIES MOVING ABROAD

Some locally-based companies might decide to re-locate their business overseas, to have a better chance of their business being successful. The reasons for this may include:

- There is less tax to pay to the government.

- The local people are prepared to work for lower wages.

- Supplies and raw materials can be purchased more cheaply.

- The running costs of the business are overall much lower.

This will have an effect on the local job market as when a business moves overseas, the existing employees will be made redundant and left facing unemployment.

ACTIVITY

Work in groups of about 4.

Use the Internet or newspapers to investigate job advertisements.

- What types of work are available in your local area and in Northern Ireland?

Use the Internet to research local companies that have chosen to re-locate overseas.

- What type of businesses are they?

- Why have they moved abroad?

Present your findings to the rest of the class.

1. Write a short paragraph to explain how employment has changed in Northern Ireland over the last 50 years or so.

2. What trends seem likely for the future, regarding:

   a) the type of jobs people do.

   b) where people work.

   c) the hours people work.

MIGRATION AND IMMIGRATION

Not everyone is fortunate enough to find suitable employment in their local area – for many people finding work means moving, perhaps even to a foreign country. Traditionally, far more people have left Northern Ireland than have arrived looking for work. In recent years, the situation has changed and there are now a significant number of new citizens, particularly from other parts of the European Union.

Migration

This means to move from one place to another, usually looking for more favourable conditions. Migration can be short or long-term. Short-term migration might be seasonal as people (and birds and animals) move because of climate. Seasonal migration can affect people who are looking for work, as temporary opportunities become available, for example, farming work.

Emigration

This is a more permanent move than migration. Emigration is the act of leaving a country permanently to live elsewhere. In the past, many people have emigrated from Northern Ireland to live in America, Australia and other parts of the UK.

Immigration

This is also a permanent move of people. Immigration is when new citizens come into a particular area, rather than leaving it. Immigrants to Northern Ireland include people from China, India and more recently from Eastern Europe.

MIGRANT WORKERS IN NORTHERN IRELAND

Who is a migrant worker?

A migrant worker is a person who travels to a different area looking for work. Unlike immigrants, they have not necessarily come here to stay permanently, although many of them do eventually settle. It is worth remembering that most people living in Northern Ireland probably have a migrant worker in their family!

Where do many migrant workers come from?

Migrant workers in Northern Ireland include people of European nationality from countries such as Portugal or Italy, who have a right to live and work anywhere in the UK. People from Eastern Europe started arriving in 2004 after countries such as Poland and Latvia joined the EU. Eastern Europeans must register on the Workers Registration Scheme. Migrant workers from the Philippines can be employed in Northern Ireland, but a local employer must obtain a work permit.

Migrant workers come to Northern Ireland as they are hoping for employment opportunities, or perhaps the chance to start a business. Some are recruited by employment agencies.

What problems do migrant workers face?

Migrant workers are becomingly increasingly significant in Northern Ireland and make a valuable contribution to the economy and cultural life. However, they often experience harassment and abuse, both in the workplace and on the streets. Some people feel that migrant workers are "taking our jobs" but in reality there is a shortage of labour in some areas of the employment market. Many migrant workers are employed in the food processing industry or agriculture, often doing back-breaking work for low pay. Migrant workers are often at a disadvantage and easily exploited because of language difficulties. There have been cases where migrant workers have had to pay a large amount of their wages on very poor accommodation provided by the recruitment agency.

Compile a table of key points to show the difficulties and opportunities facing migrant workers in Northern Ireland.

- Discuss your findings with others in the class.
- How might the difficulties be overcome?

CASE STUDY: STEP (SOUTH TYRONE EMPOWERMENT PROGRAMME)

STEP provides community development and training services to individuals and organisations in the South Tyrone community and across Northern Ireland.

STEP Migrant Workers' Support Project has been operating since 2001 when employees and other individuals volunteered advice and guidance for Migrant Workers coming to the Dungannon area.

The following example shows how STEP supports migrant workers:

In November 2005, STEP was contacted by a young Latvian couple with an eight month old baby. Their employer, a recruitment agency, expected the family to share a room with a single bed in a three-bedroomed house in which six other Latvian men also resided. The couple were paying £120 per week for a room which was cold and damp. When they complained to their employer, they were told they would be evicted and lose their jobs if they complained again. STEP contacted the landlord and asked for the family to be moved to more suitable accommodation. The family were eventually moved to a two-bedroom flat, and stayed a short time before finding alternative accommodation with another agency.

Source: 'Migrant Workers in Northern Ireland', Concordia Partnership, www.concordiapartnership.org, p7

Text cannot be reprinted without permission from STEP. For further information visit: www.stepni.org

RESEARCH ACTIVITY

Use the Internet to find a story of a person who has come to Northern Ireland looking for work. Find out the reasons why they left their home country and why they came to Northern Ireland.

EMIGRATION FROM NORTHERN IRELAND

Why do people emigrate from Northern Ireland? There are many reasons why a person might choose to emigrate, such as:

- **Religious or political reasons** – In some parts of the world, a person's life could be in danger because of their beliefs and they may be forced to flee from their country because of persecution. While this does not happen in Northern Ireland, during 'the Troubles' many people chose to leave as they were fed up with the violence and sectarianism.

- **Economic reasons or job opportunities** – Some people feel that Northern Ireland lacks opportunities for business or employment. By moving overseas they can have a better job with higher pay and therefore enjoy a better standard of living. Sometimes people who emigrate for economic reasons do eventually return home, perhaps after they have earned sufficient money in the other country.

- **Health or personal reasons** – A person might emigrate because of marriage, moving to the country their partner is from, or perhaps joining other family members already living there. Some people enjoy a warm climate or feel it is better for their health and may move to a sunnier country when they retire.

Is emigration good for the economy?

On one hand, you might think that emigration will have positive effects as it takes some people out of the job market. However, if the people who are leaving are those with training and skills then the result can be a '**brain drain**'. This means there are too many unskilled workers, while posts for people with specific skills cannot be filled.

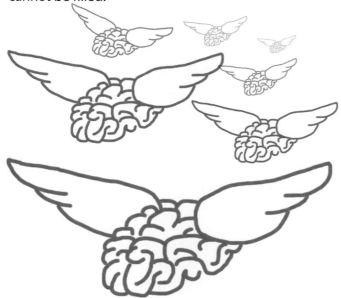

How do the people involved feel about the move? If a whole family is emigrating, perhaps because of a parent's work, then not everyone may be excited about the move. The children in the family may find it hard to adjust and miss their friends and school. Grandparents back home might be anxious that they will miss out on seeing their grandchildren growing up.

How does the host country feel about new citizens? Some governments welcome professional people coming to live and work in their country as they have a shortage of skilled workers. Other workers in the new country may not be so welcoming, particularly if there is competition for jobs.

"My son and his wife emigrated to New Zealand shortly after they were married. They love it and say they have a much better quality of life over there, with better promotion prospects. I miss my grandchildren, though, as I don't get to see them very often."

"I can't wait to go to university. I'm getting out of this place and I'll not be back! There are much better opportunities across the water."

- Do you know anyone who has moved away from Northern Ireland?
- What reason did they have for leaving?
- Has the move been a successful one for them?

GROWTH OF NEW TECHNOLOGIES

TECHNOLOGY IN DAILY LIFE

Can you imagine life with no mobile phone, computer or Internet, games console or even no television? Your grandparents, and possibly your parents, might remember what it was like not to have some of them. However, for many of us today these things are an essential part of daily life. New technology has an impact on everyone, whether you are keeping in touch with friends, revising for exams, shopping or just relaxing at home.

ACTIVITY

Work in groups of about 3 or 4.

- Create a spider diagram of the different technologies you use everyday, at home and at school.
- Discuss the impact that these have had on your everyday life.

Here is an example:

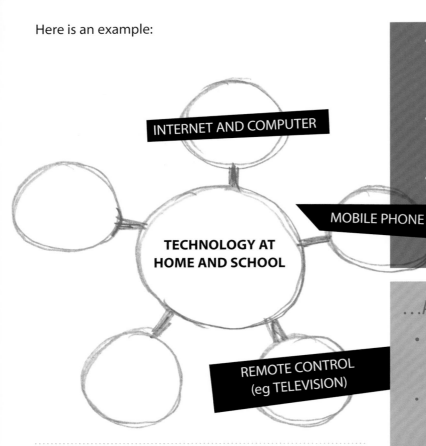

INTERNET AND COMPUTER

TECHNOLOGY AT HOME AND SCHOOL

MOBILE PHONE

REMOTE CONTROL (eg TELEVISION)

- **Higher profits and a higher income** – This is due to the increase in efficiency and production, combined with the need for less staff.
- **Advanced communications** – These include the use of email, mobile phones and computer systems.
- **A more competitive business** – Some of the savings made through the new technology can be used to lower prices and attract more customers.

...AND SOME DISADVANTAGES...

- **New skills** – Employees may have to be re-trained so they can operate the new technology.
- **Maintenance** – The new equipment may be difficult to maintain. If it breaks down, will the whole work schedule be affected?
- **Costs** – The new technology may be very expensive to install at the start, even though it may save money in the long-term.
- **Time** – It may take time to re-organise the workplace to set up the new technology. A business working to very tight deadlines may find this is impractical.

TECHNOLOGY IN THE WORKPLACE

Technology is changing the workplace, having an impact on both the work that is carried out and the way in which it is done. Technology has led to many positive changes, but also presents some challenges. It can make the workplace efficient and effective, but employees at all levels have to be confident using it. A business needs to decide at what point it needs to upgrade to the latest technology or whether this may be impractical as too many staff will have to be re-trained. Some businesses do not need the latest technology to help them move forwards and be successful.

ADVANTAGES OF TECHNOLOGY FOR A BUSINESS...

- **An increase in productivity** – new technology can allow jobs to be completed more quickly.
- **Fewer employees are needed** – Many jobs that needed employees can now be automated.

Some examples of technology in business

- **Retailing** – Many businesses are using the Internet as a way of promoting their products or giving customers the opportunity to shop online. Designing and managing 'virtual stores' is becoming a top priority for large retailers. Many large stores use computer software to keep a check on stock levels.

- **Manufacturing** – New technology has helped manufacturers to make products more quickly and cheaply. This includes machine tools, design software and the use of IT to keep in contact with suppliers and customers.
- **Agriculture** – Farmers are now using satellites and IT to support precision farming. This involves collecting data to find out which part of their land is best suited to certain crops, perhaps because it is drier or sunnier. The data can also inform farmers what fertilisers and pesticides a particular piece of land needs.

- **Hospitality** – Hotels now need to have the latest and best in Internet services, as this is what customers demand. Managers in the industry believe that over the next decade, the broadband speed will be a deciding factor in a guest's choice of hotel. The number of remote controlled gadgets in the room, such as coffee machine, and temperature and lighting controls will be more important than what is on the menu for breakfast!
- **Catering** – You are probably already familiar with this latest technology for the catering industry, as it is now also being used by many schools:

ITOUCH FOR CASHLESS CATERING

iTouch software is the ideal cashless catering system for any school or business that provides students or staff with a catering facility. iTouch's features have been designed specifically for the corporate and education markets to improve meal time administration and operational efficiency. A cashless catering system greatly improves security and can also boost food sales, which means more profit is generated.

The key aim of the iTouch Cashless Catering EPOS system is to make lunch times more efficient and to remove the need for staff and students to carry money by instead using their fingerprint, swipe, proximity or smart card as a method of payment.

Information taken from http://www.rstepos.com/

THE IMPACT OF TECHNOLOGY ON EMPLOYMENT

Technology is changing employment, whether the workplace is a dairy farm, office or restaurant. This has created both opportunities and challenges for businesses in Northern Ireland.

Changing skills

The growing use of technology and development of new equipment has led to the creation of many new areas of employment. The ICT industry, in particular, is expected to see significant growth over the next decade, with many new areas for employment created. Businesses need to employ people who are trained and proficient in the use of new technologies, and also need to motivate existing staff to acquire new skills. Employees need to be flexible and willing to re-train so they can use new equipment.

Redundancies and unemployment

Technology leads to more automation of tasks and less need for people to be employed to do them, which is one of the reasons why using new technologies can save businesses money. An example of this is in the banking sector, where the introduction of telephone and Internet banking had led to many large banks closing their high street branches. Does this mean that as computers and machines are replacing human workers there is going to be more unemployment? The situation is not quite as simple as that and the introduction of new technology does not always lead to redundancies. Improved technology can reduce costs and can lead to more competitive prices. This could lead to an increased demand for a product, which might require more workers being hired.

evaluation

Evaluate the impact that new technology has had in the workplace.

RESEARCH ACTIVITY

Work in groups of about 3 or 4. Choose one industry in Northern Ireland and research what jobs are available.

- Are there many opportunities within this sector of employment?
- What types of jobs are available and what skills are needed?

EMPLOYEES WITH DISABILITIES

New computer technology is now being developed for the workplace to help employees who are disabled. This is called assistive technology. Many jobs nowadays require IT skills, yet for some disabled people this can be a barrier to employment as standard equipment can be difficult for them to use. Assistive technology can make computers accessible for a person who is disabled, or simply makes their working life easier. This opens up new opportunities for a section of the population who have often been overlooked in the workplace.

Here are some examples:

- A person who is physically impaired may find it difficult to use a standard keyboard or mouse, but there are many alternatives available. These include one-handed keyboards and screen pointers, which can be controlled with almost any part of the body.
- Voice recognition software is available, which may be helpful for people with a physical disability or who are visually impaired. This software turns speech into text.
- An employee who is partially sighted could try magnification software. This enables a person to zoom in and enlarge what is on the computer screen.

- Special screen reading software has been developed so people who are blind can use computers. Words on the screen are converted into speech and a braille readout can also be produced on a special display under the keyboard.

ACTIVITY

Write a description for a new job that you think may be available in around 10 years time.

Try to imagine what skills and qualifications this position will need.

What will be the hours of work?

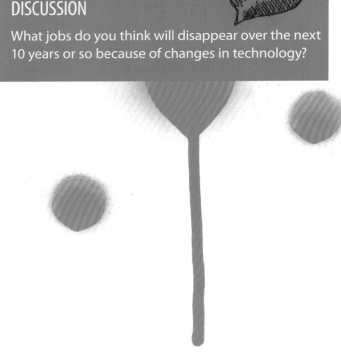

DISCUSSION

What jobs do you think will disappear over the next 10 years or so because of changes in technology?

EXAM FOCUS

This section will appear at the end of every chapter. It will help you to develop your exam skills.

As well as covering different topics, your exam will also have different types of question testing different skills. One of these skills is to **demonstrate your knowledge and understanding.**

The following question tests this skill:

(a) Name *two* imports to Northern Ireland. [2 marks]

(b) Identify and explain *two* ways in which global trading can bring benefits to people living in Northern Ireland. [4 marks]

(c) Identify and explain *two* ways in which technology can help a business to be successful. [4 marks]

When answering part (b) and part (c) of this question, start by clearly stating what you are going to write about, then give your explanation.

You could begin part (b) in the following way:

"Greater choice for consumers – We enjoy foods that cannot be produced in Northern Ireland as the climate is not suitable, such as coffee, oranges and bananas. Global trading gives us variety in what we eat and a better standard of living."

Continue this answer adding an example of your own. Write your own answer for Part (c).

Chapter two

RECRUITMENT AND SELECTION PRACTICES FOR EMPLOYMENT

CHAPTER SUMMARY

In this chapter you will be studying:

- **The importance of lifelong learning.**
- **The competencies and personal qualities valued by employers.**
- **How to make a successful application.**
- **What is meant by 'Employability'.**

INTRODUCTION

What is it that makes someone successful in employment, from the initial application and interview to promotion opportunities? It is not just a matter of luck, although sometimes a person can manage to be in the right place at the right time!

There are a number of skills and qualities that employers look for. Having the right qualifications is vital but personal qualities are also very important. From the moment you first make contact with a prospective employer you will be giving an impression of yourself. Is it the right impression? Once a person is employed, it is also important to make sure that skills are kept up-to-date as there are many changes happening in the world of work. All of this can be summarised into one word – **Employability**.

LIFELONG LEARNING

Learning is not just for school, when you work for your exams, it is a continual process that takes place throughout a person's life. Once someone is in employment, then the learning process will also involve professional development and acquiring new work-related skills. This is known as lifelong learning. Chapter one looked at some of the ways in which the workplace is changing. The successful employee is someone who is flexible and well-equipped to face change, with relevant skills and up-to-date training. Investing some time in learning new skills means equipping yourself for the future, as you will have a better chance of gaining promotion or changing careers.

Career advancement can mean different things for different people. For some, it can mean climbing up the promotion ladder as quickly as possible; for some it is important for them simply to do their job well and get recognition for this. However you see your career path, lifelong learning is important.

THE ADVANTAGES OF LIFELONG LEARNING

Some of the advantages of lifelong learning in the context of work can be seen in the spider diagram below.

- DEVELOP EXISTING SKILLS
- ACQUIRE NEW SKILLS
- GREATER JOB SATISFACTION
- **LIFELONG LEARNING**
- RAISE SELF-ESTEEM
- GAIN FURTHER QUALIFICATIONS
- BECOME MORE MOTIVATED

On the other hand, it is worth remembering that there is a level of commitment involved in lifelong learning. Deciding to study for further qualifications or learn new skills may not be easy and takes time and effort.

Here are some important questions a person will need to consider:

- How much will it cost, and will my employer help meet some of these expenses?
- Will I have to sacrifice time spent with friends and family?
- Will my new skills or qualifications lead to career development or promotion?
- Do I have the time for this new course, without becoming too stressed or fatigued because of existing commitments?

ACTIVITY

In small groups, discuss the advantages and disadvantages of lifelong learning. Can you think of any others?

WHAT IS A CAREER PLAN?

A career plan is a road map that helps you reach your destination – your chosen long-term goals. On a journey, a map will help you decide what turning to take and what direction to follow. A career plan works in a similar way when you have important choices to make. For example, what subjects should I choose to study? Will I stay on at school for AS and A2 levels? Will I think of applying for university or a course at a college of further education? Questions such as these will be easier to answer if you have a career plan and you know the goal you are aiming for.

Career planning does not stop once you get a job – like learning, it is a lifelong process. It is important for a person to grow and develop in their chosen occupation and this may involve re-training or changing jobs.

A career plan is important because it helps a person take control of where they are going in the world of work. If you have clear goals, both long and short-term, it can help you to focus and be motivated to achieve them. Drifting from one idea to another, unsure of what you want to do, is less likely to bring career success.

ACTIVITY

Make a career plan for yourself.

- Go back to when you first started to think about a career or make choices, such as which subjects you chose to study for GCSE.

- Go as far forward as you possibly can.

- You might like to present your plan as a flow diagram or road map showing where you intend to go.

TRAINING COURSES

Most employers will recognise that lifelong learning is important and that it is better for business if employees are well equipped with relevant skills. Some training takes place within the normal working environment, using the tools and equipment that are part of the job. This is known as **on-the-job training**. Sometimes employees will be trained outside the workplace, perhaps at a local College of Further Education. This is known as **off-the-job training**.

Training courses can bring benefits to both the employer and employee. Here are some examples:

- The employee gains up-to-date knowledge and skills which will benefit the organisation.

- Employees can become more motivated which will lead to greater efficiency in their work.

- Gaining new skills means that employees can carry out different tasks, which means that their work can become more effective.

- Employees who are highly trained are more efficient in their work and this can enhance the opportunity for promotion.

- If employees are trained in health and safety procedures this can decrease the possibility of accidents in the workplace. It is better for the business if there are less staff absent from work due to work-related injuries.

THE 'CREDIT CRUNCH' AND UNEMPLOYMENT

The economic downturn of 2008 had a global impact, from the large, multi-national companies to small, local businesses. When money is lost, cut-backs have to be made and this often means that people lose their jobs as a result. Northern Ireland has had a long-term problem with unemployment, with statistics showing that this is often the most seriously affected region in the whole of the UK. Although there has been some improvement since the 'credit crunch', unemployment is still a cause for concern. When people are unemployed or facing redundancy, they may need to be flexible and make changes.

These might include:

- Re-training
- Changing job
- Moving to a different area
- Studying for a qualification

ACTIVITY

Survey the other students in your class.

- Does anyone have a family member who has re-trained or changed their career?
- What was the reason for this?

NEWS ITEM

ANOTHER RISE IN NORTHERN IRELAND UNEMPLOYMENT RATE

The number of people claiming unemployment benefits in Northern Ireland rose again in June.

The number claiming jobless benefits was 56,100, a rise of 600 on the figures for May. The claimant count has now gone up by 13.6% in the past year. Analysis by the Ulster Bank indicates that by 2012 the number of jobless will have trebled over five years.

Unemployment in Northern Ireland rose despite a fall of 34,000 across the rest of the UK. Enterprise minister Arlene Foster said she was disappointed because claimant levels had remained "fairly static" over the first five months of the year. She added that the NI economy was likely to face further pressures because of impending public spending cuts.

Richard Ramsey, Ulster Bank chief economist, agreed that spending reduction would have a significant impact on the economy in NI, leading to job losses both in the public sector and areas of the private sector that rely on public expenditure. He also warned that forthcoming cuts in incapacity and welfare benefits would see more individuals move out of economic inactivity back into unemployment. "Northern Ireland can expect its dole queue to lengthen significantly as result," he added.

The Labour Force Survey suggests that the current rate of economic inactivity in Northern Ireland is 26.4%. Northern Ireland's rate of economic inactivity, defined by those who are not in employment but are not actively seeking jobs, is the highest in the UK, 5.2% more than the nationwide average.

Source: 'Another rise in Northern Ireland unemployment rate', BBC News, 14 July 2010, http://www.bbc.co.uk/news/10629445

ACTIVITY

Read the news item above.

How would you reply to the comment below? Be positive!

> "Unemployment is going up again! What is the point of even bothering with qualifications or work experience only to end up in a dole queue?"

FINDING OUT ABOUT OPPORTUNITIES

There are a number of organisations in Northern Ireland offering opportunities for further learning. There is a range of different courses available to help people prepare for work, up-date or improve their existing skills, change careers or go back to work following a career break.

Institutes of Further and Higher Education

Northern Ireland's 16 Further Education Colleges merged into 6 larger and more influential colleges in 2007. They provide a wide range of courses, from basic literacy and numeracy up to degree level.

The new colleges are:

- Belfast Metropolitan College – Greater Belfast and Castlereagh.
- Northern Regional College – The Coleraine area and County Antrim.
- North West Regional College – Londonderry and Limavady areas.
- South Eastern Regional College – North and East County Down.
- Southern Regional College – The Newry area and County Armagh.
- South West College – Counties Tyrone and Fermanagh.

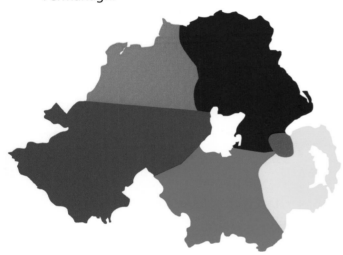

Learn Direct

Learn Direct offer a range of courses in Maths, English, IT, business and management. Their courses are designed to help people get on at work, improve their CV or increase the chance of getting a job. All the learning is done online, so all that is needed is access to the Internet. Learners can study when and where they like, at a pace that suits them. Learn Direct work with Colleges of Further and Higher Education in Northern Ireland and have also introduced the 'Internet Made Easy' drop-in sessions to libraries throughout Northern Ireland.

Job Centres

The local Jobs and Benefits office or JobCentre is a good starting place for a person who is looking for a job or who wants to get back to work. Their Careers and Guidance Services can give advice on a range of education and training options. (See page 72, Chapter four for more information.)

Careers Service Northern Ireland

Careers Advisers are based in JobCentres and Careers Offices throughout Northern Ireland. They provide help and guidance to all people of all ages, so they can make informed choices about their future career path. Careers Advisers may visit schools, often in years 10 and 12, when important decisions have to be made. They work alongside careers teachers in schools, to give additional help.

'Next Step' is a new careers service especially for adults. Next Step advisers will give guidance over the phone or in a face-to face interview, helping people make the right choices about learning and work.

Educational Guidance Service for Adults (EGSA)

EGSA is a local, independent, non-profit making service that aims to connect adults with learning. It has a network of local offices throughout Northern Ireland and provides services to adult learners, learning advisers and employers.

EGSA give support to employees by helping them explore career options. This is done by phone, email or interview. Advice may be given on how to:

- Create a personal action plan.
- Improve English, Maths or Computer Skills.
- Develop new skills and gain qualifications.
- Use career matching software.

EGSA support employers by offering a package of services aimed at helping them through economic change. EGSA can deliver advice sessions and consultations to employers who are faced with having to make staff redundant. Employers can then advise their staff on training options and how to make the most of their employment potential.

QUALIFICATIONS AVAILABLE

There are a variety of different qualifications available, at different levels.

- Academic qualifications involve learning and study of a particular area of knowledge, for example, GCSE History.

- Applied qualifications require academic study with some application to a particular area of work, for example, AS Level Health and Social Care.

- Vocational qualifications are primarily involved with the practical skills and knowledge needed to carry out a particular job, for example, a BTEC qualification in 3D Design.

GCSEs

You are probably studying for GCSEs at the moment. GCSEs are mainly academic, with some applied subjects. They are valued highly by colleges of further education and employers, so your GCSEs will be useful whatever you are planning to do in your future career.

AS and A2 Levels

AS (Advanced Subsidiary) and A2 (Advanced) level qualifications are usually offered to Students in Sixth Form at school. There are a wide range of academic subjects available as well as some applied subjects. AS and A2 Levels are one of the main routes into higher education but can also be useful for some jobs, such as office administration.

Diplomas

A diploma is a qualification for 14–19 year olds, combining practical training with academic learning. There is a wide choice of diplomas available, such as Hair and Beauty Studies, and Sport and Active Leisure.

BTECs and City and Guilds

BTEC (Business and Technology Education Council) awards and City and Guilds qualifications are available in a range of subjects. They are closely linked to industry and are designed to give the practical skills that employers are looking for. These qualifications also involve work experience and are often taken as part of an apprenticeship.

Foundation Degrees

A Foundation Degree is a university-level qualification, but designed with a particular area of work in mind. They are suitable for people of all ages and backgrounds, and can be particularly useful if someone wants a career change or to increase their prospects of promotion.

NVQs, HNCs and HNDs

An NVQ (National Vocational Qualification) can be completed while in full-time education, or as part of a job or apprenticeship. A wide variety of practical courses are available, such as plumbing, hairdressing and social care. HNCs (Higher National Certificates) and HNDs (Higher National Diplomas) are vocational higher education qualifications. They focus on the professional skills rather than academic knowledge and are provided by universities and further education colleges. HNCs usually take one year to complete full time, while HNDs take two years. Some of the subjects available include agriculture, computing and engineering.

BA and BSc Degrees

A bachelors degree is a course of academic study in arts-based subjects, such as English (BA), or science-based subjects, such as physics or computing (BSc). They are designed to give a thorough knowledge and understanding of a particular subject.

Postgraduate qualifications

These qualifications are for people who want to continue studying after completing a bachelors degree. They give the opportunity for someone to work independently and carry out an original piece of research.

CHECK YOUR LEARNING

1. Explain what is meant by 'lifelong learning'.
2. Why is lifelong learning important?
3. What is a career plan?
4. What are the advantages of a career plan?
5. Explain the importance of:

    a) Training

    b) Qualifications

    c) Careers advice

CASE STUDY: MARK LAIRD FOUNDATION DEGREE IN COMPUTING

A career change can be daunting, but Mark is confident of reaching his potential – with the help of a flexible Foundation Degree …

After working for 16 years in factories and as a technician, Mark wanted a change. He chose to study Computing. After starting a Higher National Certificate (HNC) course, he switched to a Foundation Degree.

Mark felt that Lancaster University's Foundation Degree offered flexibility, real-world computing experience and the right environment for him.

"The modules were up-to-date and highly applicable to future work", he explains, "Equally, the complete mix of students and locality of study were important considerations. Overall it was a very supportive environment, especially for more mature learners. The system was very flexible, with a choice of lectures at the beginning or end of the week – with nursery and crèche facilities for those who needed them".

Mark's work placement saw him developing software in a local travel agency. "It gave me far more technical knowledge than I might have gained elsewhere", he says. The placement also gave him an understanding of customers' needs in the real world. "I was regularly speaking and communicating with managing directors and got a really invaluable insight into business at a higher level."

Since completing the Foundation Degree, Mark has "got the education bug". He took a BSc at Blackburn, and now he is working towards an MSc at Lancaster. "I might go on to do a PhD: I haven't decided," he says. "Either way, I think I stand a great chance of achieving my goal of working for an established software house."

Source: © Crown copyright, http://www.direct.gov.uk/en/EducationAndLearning/QualificationsExplained/DG_186148

COMPETENCIES AND PERSONAL QUALITIES

Some jobs require specific skills and employers will be looking for people who have the right training and qualifications. An employee's competencies are the things they are good at – the skills, abilities and personality traits that help to make them successful at work. Some of these skills will be **transferable skills**, meaning they are not related to a specific occupation. They are the skills a person has gained through various jobs or voluntary work, hobbies and sports and other life experiences. Transferable skills are important, whether a person is starting a new job, changing career, facing redundancy or re-entering the world of work after a long absence, perhaps to raise a family.

Many of the transferable skills that employers are looking for fall into one of the following categories:

Essential skills

Essential skills, or key skills, refer to skills that are needed in many different situations – whether at school, in training, at work or as part of daily life.

These skills include:

- Literacy
- Numeracy
- ICT

Critical, creative and problem-solving skills

Many employers are starting to place increasing value on these skills. They show that an employee will be able to handle a variety of different tasks and situations in the workplace, and be able to offer a new approach.

These skills include:

- Creativity
- Decision making
- Problem Solving
- Flexibility
- Time management

Personal skills

A person's relationship with their colleagues can be very important in creating a pleasant working environment. Good relations in the workplace can help everyone to do their job better and make going to work everyday enjoyable. This is one of the reasons why personal skills or qualities are so important. In addition to this, the workplace today can be very competitive. A person with a variety of skills, who can get on well with others will have a competitive edge.

These skills include:

- Commitment
- Loyalty
- Working well with others
- Honesty
- Discipline
- Enthusiasm
- Motivation

ACTIVITY

Many employers are choosing to use the Internet to advertise their employment vacancies. Some examples have been included below.

For each of the jobs advertised describe the following:

- The skills and personal qualities the employer is looking for.
- Any additional skills not mentioned in the advertisement that you think would be an asset to the post.

CARE ASSISTANT IN A NURSING HOME

Job Duties: Care of elderly residents, aiding with their daily needs, dressing, washing, feeding, etc.

Experience: Experience preferred. Training will be given.

Hours: Full-time, shift pattern, day or night, 7 days a week.

PLAYGROUP ASSISTANT

Job Duties: Working with children in a play environment. We are looking for fun, flexible and motivated staff who love working with children. Must be aged 16 or over.

Desirable skills:

- Good Communication skills with children and adults.
- Ability to work well as a member of a team.
- Flexibility.
- Ability to cope in difficult or stressful situations.
- Genuine interest in children and welfare issues.

Hours: Part-time, mornings only.

MACHINE OPERATOR IN A FACTORY

Job Duties: To carry out a variety of activities within the production process. The applicant will enable production requirements to be met in the most effective and efficient manner and ensure orders are met on time.

Hours: 12 hour shifts, working 36 hours per week.

RETAIL ASSISTANT

Job Duties: Dealing with customers on the shop floor, general office duties, answering telephones, taking orders, helping customers, dispatching orders to customers and any other duties that would be required in a medium sized business.

Experience: Computer experience desirable.

Hours: Full time, 9–5 Mon–Fri, plus one late night per week.

WHAT ARE 'SOFT SKILLS'?

As well as education and experience, many employers are also looking for a range of personal skills. The term 'soft skills' refers to qualities such as team work, using your initiative and communication. These are now seen as being increasingly important to help both business and relationships run smoothly. Soft skills do not come with a formal qualification. They are either part of a person's personal qualities or they can be learnt through practical experience. Many companies have now realised that these skills are important and are spending money to make sure employees have them. A person who proves that they have well developed soft skills may well stand a better chance when applying for jobs or going for promotion.

DISCUSSION

What do you think are the most important competencies and qualities valued by employers? Give reasons for your opinion.

ACTIVITY

Work in pairs.

- Collect some examples of job advertisements from newspapers or the Internet.
- Decide what you think are the personal qualities and competencies needed for each job.
- Share your ideas with the rest of the class.

HOW WILL AN EMPLOYER ASSESS COMPETENCIES AND PERSONAL QUALITIES?

Your application for a job will say a lot about you, not just through the information you choose to give, but the way you present it. An employer might assess personal qualities and skills through:

- An initial telephone call
- Correspondence through letter or email
- The application form
- The interview
- An assessment, such as a presentation or test

First impressions can be vital. It will be important to show that you can communicate well; speak clearly, write concisely and do not forget to use the spell checker on your computer!

THE SUCCESSFUL CANDIDATE

THE IMPORTANCE OF CAREERS ADVICE

The number of different careers to choose from can be exciting, but at the same time rather daunting. Also, many people (parents and teachers) seem to think you will already have your mind made up about what you want to do. That's fine if you have, but it can be very confusing if you are still not sure. This is why it is very important to take careers advice seriously. Careers Advisers and Careers teachers in school are knowledgeable about the current employment situation and further education. They are experienced in giving advice and can help you to make important choices.

A careers teacher in school can help students to make decisions about their careers in some of the following ways:

- Students can discuss their likes and dislikes and their personal capabilities. Their careers teacher can then give advice on the jobs or courses that would suit them best.

- Careers teachers will be knowledgeable in all aspects of post 16 or post 18 courses and can suggest a course that is realistic. A teacher will be aware of what exams you are working towards in school and what you could aim for next.

- Careers teachers can give impartial advice to students so they are equipped to make their own decisions about their future.

RESEARCH ACTIVITY

Use the Internet to research the job or career you would like to do. If you don't know what job you would like to do but have a few ideas, research a few different careers. It might help you to know a bit more about them.

- Find out what additional training or qualifications you will need.

- Are there any additional skills or personal capabilities needed?

- Are there plenty of opportunities in Northern Ireland or will you need to think about moving away in the future?

WORK EXPERIENCE

Work experience is another important factor which will help with future career planning. A work placement is the opportunity to spend some time in a place of employment and discover more about a career or job. You will be able to find out about what skills are

needed and may have the opportunity to practice some of these. Talking to people who already do a particular job can help you decide whether this employment really is for you. Many schools arrange work experience for their students, either in years 11 or 12 or in Sixth Form. Make the most of any opportunity you get for work experience as it can help you make important choices about career plans. You can also gain valuable experience to use in future applications for courses or employment.

"I learnt a lot from my work experience. I always thought I wanted to work with young children … until I spent a week in a playgroup! It put me off completely and I am now working as a secretary in a solicitor's office."

"I have always loved animals. When I was about 14 I started to help out on Saturday mornings at a local kennels. When I was 16 I got a part-time job at my local stables. I also made sure I had at least one placement at the local vets or with a farmer lined up during the summer holidays. Without this work experience I wouldn't have got a place at university to study veterinary medicine. It gives you that competitive edge and shows that you have a genuine interest in something."

YOUR CURRICULUM VITAE

A Curriculum Vitae (CV) is a summary of a person's education and employment history, giving details of qualifications, training and experience. Employers might ask for a CV to be submitted to support a job application, to help them decide if you are the sort of person they are looking for. Some people keep their CV up-to-date even if they are not actively job seeking as it can be useful to have all this information together in one place. It could also be needed if applying for promotion within a company.

Today, many job applications are made online, so if your CV is stored electronically it can easily be emailed. It is worth remembering that a prospective employer might make a judgement about a person from the initial impression given by their CV – so it is important to take time over producing yours to get it right.

Your careers teacher in school may give you advice on how to write a CV, but here are some basic guidelines:

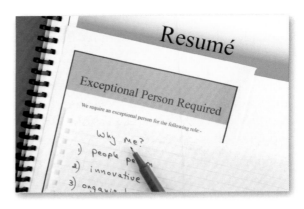

- Word process your CV and use a clear font. Do not be tempted to produce a multi-coloured document and do not use fancy borders and layout.

- Keep it short – your CV should be no more than two sides of A4 paper.

- Start with your name, address and other contact details.

- Give the names of schools you have attended, with dates.

- Include any awards, achievements or qualifications you have gained.

- Refer to any work experience you have. This could be a placement organised by your school or any experience gained from a part time job.

- Mention personal qualities, such as your skills and strengths, and refer to hobbies and interests that you enjoy in your spare time.

- Stick to the truth – do not be tempted to invent or exaggerate. On the other hand, do not be critical of yourself. Keep to positive statements and write truthfully.

- You may wish to change some of the details in your CV to make it more relevant for a particular application. There may be something that you wish to expand on to show your suitability for the post.

- Include the names and contact details of two people (not relatives) who would be willing to supply a reference to a prospective employer. It is a courtesy to ask their permission beforehand.

- If you are sending a paper copy of your CV make sure it is printed clearly on good quality white paper.

JANE CLARK

10 Hill Street, Newtown, NT17 2AW
Tel: 10234 556 789
Date of Birth: 11/12/95

Education

Newtown Primary School, Hillview Road, Newtown: September 1999–June 2006
Newtown High School, Valley Close, Newtown: September 2006–June 2011

GCSEs to be completed in June 2011: Maths, English, Science (Double Award), Drama, French, Geography, ICT, Religious Education (Short Course).

Work Experience

The Supermarket,
High Street, Newtown

Duration: Saturdays and school holidays.
Role and responsibilities: Cashier dealing with customers, stock control.

Newtown Council Offices,
Newtown

Duration: Work experience in year 11.
Role and responsibilities: Working at the reception desk, using a switchboard and computer, delivering and collecting the post.

Skills and personal qualities

I am an adaptable person. I have a good telephone manner, am confident when dealing with customers and when speaking in front of people. I have an outgoing personality, find it easy to make friends and can work well in a team. I am punctual and rarely absent from school.

Interests

I enjoy reading, dancing, swimming and hockey.

I am currently training for the Bronze Medallion in Lifesaving.

I play hockey for my school and I am on the 1st XI team.

I am a member of my local Girls' Brigade and help out at the church crèche on Sunday mornings.

References

Mr B Jones, Head of Year 12, Newtown High School, Newtown, NT16 3HS.
Ms V Smith, Manager, The Supermarket, High Street, Newtown, NT18 6SM

MAKING AN APPLICATION

When you see a job advertised that you are interested in applying for, the first stage in your application is usually to download, or request by telephone or in writing, further information. This usually includes 'essential' and 'desirable' criteria. This refers to the skills, qualifications and experience you must have in order to apply, and some of the qualities the employer might like to see. It will be important to read this

very carefully before making an application, to decide what evidence you can use to show that you meet the criteria.

It is important to have your CV ready when you are applying for jobs. Not all employers ask for one as part of an application, but it is still useful to have all your dates and past experiences together in one place. You may not have any difficulty remembering details at this stage, but in 10 or 20 years time it could be more of an effort!

Some places of employment will have their own application form that you need to fill in. The details asked for will probably be similar to the information on your CV. As with your CV, it is important that your application form is filled in neatly and clearly, with no spelling or grammar mistakes. If you have a paper form to fill in, rather than an online version, draft what you are going to write beforehand to avoid the need for tippex and crossing out. Take careful note of any instructions that are given with the application form. You might be asked to use black pen, for example, as the form is to be photocopied for other people on the interview panel.

Application forms may have a space for you to give a personal statement outlining why you are interested in the position and how you meet the advertised criteria. It is especially important to write this carefully and include as much relevant information as you can. If you are making an application by CV, you will probably need to send a covering letter as well. In this letter you could include a brief personal statement about your suitability for the post.

EXAMPLE OF A COVERING LETTER

78 Chestnut Drive
Greenwood
GR34 5OD

Mr A Smith
The Personnel Manager
IT Solutions
Greenwood Business Park
Greenwood
GR22 7BP

19.06.2011

Dear Mr Smith

Sales Assistant

I am writing about the job of Sales Assistant with IT Solutions that is currently advertised online.

I have been interested in a career in retailing for some time and computing is one of my interests. I was attracted by your advertisement as the job offers training which I am keen to do.

For the last six months I have had a part-time job in Greenwood Electrical Superstore, working Saturdays and one evening a week. I have enjoyed this work very much. I worked in The Department Store during my work experience last year, which was organised by my school. In both jobs I had to dress smartly and be helpful and polite to customers. My experience in retailing has helped me decide that I would definitely like to make this my career. At Greenwood Electrical I have used computer software to help with the stocktaking.

I enjoy meeting and talking to people. I am reliable and my attendance at school and for my part-time job has been excellent.

My CV is enclosed, as requested.

Yours sincerely

John Jones

John Jones

INTERVIEW TECHNIQUES

There may be hundreds of applications for a job and from these a very small number will be short listed for interview. So, if you have made it to this stage there is something about your application that has interested a potential employer. Be positive about the interview and make your best effort!

Before the interview

- **Research** – Find out as much as you can about the organisation. If you know about their line of work, customers, areas where they operate or the ethos of the company, this may help when answering questions in the interview. Make sure you are fully informed about the job you are applying for, including any additional duties or responsibilities.

- **Prepare** – Consider what you know about the company, the job and the skills they are looking for. Think of some possible questions you might be asked and prepare answers. For some interviews, you will be asked to give a short talk or presentation. If so, you will be told beforehand, so obviously this will need to be prepared carefully.

- **Plan** – There are practical matters to take into consideration, to avoid the stress of a last minute rush. Plan what you are going to wear and how you are going to travel to the interview.

At the interview

- **Create a good impression** – Be aware of body language. Smile (but do not have a constant grin on your face), do not slouch or fidget with things. Remember to make eye contact during your interview and if you are being interviewed by more than one person try to address the whole panel. How you dress is very important at an interview and can go a long way towards helping

to create a positive impression. It might be a good idea to think about investing in a decent suit for interviews – definitely no jeans or trainers should be worn.

- **Draw on personal experience** – When asked questions try to answer clearly and accurately. Give examples to support what you are saying, rather than simply giving yes or no answers. Try to refer to your personal experience to give evidence that you are suitable for the post. If you do not understand a question, or think you misheard, ask the interviewer to repeat it or explain what they meant.

- **Ask any questions you may have** – Remember that an interview is also a two-way process and the person applying for the job also has to assess whether they really want it. You will probably have the opportunity to ask questions at the end of the interview.

ACTIVITY

Survey how many students in the class have part-time jobs.

- What work do they do?
- How many hours a week do they have to work?
- How did they apply for this work?
- How are they coping with part-time work and the demands of school?

DISCUSSION

Organise a class debate:

"Students who have part-time jobs are putting their school work at risk."

WHEN TO CONSIDER A CAREER CHANGE

Your application has been successful and you are now in employment! Remember that for many people today this does not mean working in the same position until you retire. There will probably be career changes along the way and new opportunities that you would like to pursue.

A change of employment may be worth considering in the following situations:

- **A change in lifestyle** – Perhaps a single person is now married with a family and wants to work more 'child friendly' hours.

- **Work has become boring** – It might be time to learn new skills or study for a qualification that will open up more opportunities.

- **The job situation has become insecure** – People in a particular area of work could be facing redundancies. Re-training for a different line of work might be sensible.

- **Not enough opportunities for promotion** – Perhaps a person feels they are not progressing fast enough in their current career. Earning more money may not necessarily bring greater job satisfaction, but having greater responsibility might.

EMPLOYABILITY

This textbook and unit of your course are on the topic of 'employability'. However, it is this chapter that really gets down to what employability is all about.

WHAT IS EMPLOYABILITY?

Employability means that you are capable of finding work in the first place, making a success of your job and being able to change careers successfully if you need to.

definitions

Employability

"Employability is about having the capability to gain initial employment, maintain employment and obtain new employment if required."*

To be successful in finding work, you need to have the right qualifications for the job and the essential skills that employers look for. It also helps if you can create a positive impression with your application right from the start. In order to do your job well and gain promotion or progress in your career, you need to have the attitude that you will continue to learn and acquire new skills. Lifelong learning is also important if you wish to change career, along with flexibility and transferable skills.

'Employability: developing a framework for policy analysis',* a research report by the Department for Education and Employment, outlines four factors on which a person's employability depends:

- Their assets – their knowledge, skills and attitudes.

- How they use these assets.

- How they present themselves to employers.

- The context in which they work – their personal circumstances and the job situation.

* Source: Hillage, J, Pollard, E, 'Employability: developing a framework for policy analysis',
Research Report RR85, Department for Education and Employment, November 1998, http://www.employment-studies.co.uk/pubs/summary.php?id=emplblty

COMPETENCIES AND PERSONAL QUALITIES FOR EMPLOYABILITY

Here are some of the factors that can help you to be a person with employability:

- Essential skills and qualifications.

- Up-to-date relevant knowledge and work related skills.

- A willingness to learn and improve.

- The ability to be flexible and adapt to new situations.

- Taking responsibility for your own career.

WHY IS EMPLOYABILITY IMPORTANT?

The person with employability is successful in employment and they are able to find satisfying work in the career of their choice. Employability is crucial as in today's world many people struggle to find work or face redundancy through no fault of their own. Make sure you have employability and an advantage over the competition!

ACTIVITY

Think about your own competencies and personal qualities.

Make a copy of the table below but leave out the examples written in each column unless you think they apply to you.

- List the qualities you have in the first column and the qualities you would like to have in the second.

Discuss your lists with a partner.

- Do you both share some of the same qualities?
- Discuss how each of you might go about gaining

the qualities you would like to have. If you can think of any solutions, write them in the third column.

If any of the qualities you have feature on your partner's 'qualities I would like to have' list (or vice versa), you might be able to help each other out!

Remember some qualities you can gain through further training, such as skills and qualifications. However, others are more to do with a change of attitude, such as adaptability and willingness to learn.

Qualities I have	Qualities I would like to have	How I could gain the qualities I would like to have
I'm good at English and can express myself well on paper.	I would like to be more confident when speaking in front of people.	Practice! I could start by volunteering to read aloud more often. I could then move on to doing presentations to the class with a group of other people, so I only have to say a few lines. Maybe by the end of the year I might be able to stand up on my own and give a short speech to the class.
I work well as part of a team and am good at taking direction.	I would like to be more confident as a team leader.	

evaluation

Evaluate the importance of employability for the twenty-first century workplace.

EXAM FOCUS

This section will appear at the end of every chapter. It will help you to develop your exam skills.

Different styles of exam question on your paper will test different skills. One of these is to show that you can **apply your knowledge and understanding.**

The following question tests this skill:

(a) Name the term used to describe training carried out in the workplace.

[1 mark]

(b) Explain **one** reason why a Curriculum Vitae (CV) needs to be constantly updated.

[2 marks]

(c) Explain **one** benefit to an employee of being trained while employed.

[2 marks]

To gain full marks for (b) and (c) you must write a detailed explanation, for example:

"A Curriculum Vitae is a record of training and employment. It should be constantly updated as a person gains new experience and learns new skills. It can then be ready for use if there is opportunity for promotion or a career change."

Question © CCEA from CCEA's GCSE Learning for Life and Work Modular Paper, Unit 5: Employability, May 2010, GLW61

oklet provided.

4 and 5.

cate the marks awarded to each

stion in allocating the available

exam

chapter three

RIGHTS AND RESPONSIBILITIES OF EMPLOYERS AND EMPLOYEES

CHAPTER SUMMARY

In this chapter you will be studying:

- The responsibilities of an employer towards an employee.
- Employment Legislation in Northern Ireland.
- How these laws affect employers and employees.
- The responsibilities of an employee towards an employer.
- The need for employers to show awareness of social and environmental issues.

INTRODUCTION

In the past, many people had to work in the most appalling conditions, working long hours in a factory or mill for very little pay. There were no adequate regulations to ensure that workers received rest breaks or did not work excessively long hours. In the country, farm labourers also worked long, hard hours for a low wage. Children worked too, some of them as young as four or five years old, doing similar tasks to the adult workers. Some children worked as chimney sweeps as they were small enough to climb up inside the chimneys of large houses. No one gave any thought to health and safety or employees rights. Accidents were common and people were often treated very badly at work.

Today, employment rights and responsibilities are crucial and ensure that employees are not exploited. Some areas of work are more dangerous than others, but employers must make efforts to minimise and control any risks. A business that values its workforce is more likely to be productive and successful, so everyone benefits. It is also important that all workers have the same protection under the law. A person's contribution to the workplace does not depend on factors such as gender, race or nationality.

THE RESPONSIBILITIES OF AN EMPLOYER

THE LAW IN NORTHERN IRELAND

It is not necessarily unlawful to treat people differently in the workplace. For example, it is common for workers to be paid different wages according to their status and skills. However, all employees must receive fair and equal treatment, and there are laws in place to ensure this. Treating people differently for some reasons may be unlawful discrimination. Employers in Northern Ireland have to comply with a wide range of general employment laws and anti-discrimination laws which aim to ensure equality at work.

Employers who provide goods, facilities or services must also ensure that they do not discriminate against customers or service users. If an employer is a public body, for example, a university, local council, hospital or government department, they have responsibilities not to discriminate. However, they also have duties to promote equality of opportunity and good relations between different groups of people. These duties are set out in Section 75 of the Northern Ireland Act which resulted from the Good Friday Agreement.

Wordbox

EQUALITY
Equality means equal rights for people regardless of how they might be different to someone else. Equality can involve both equal treatment and equal opportunity.

Equal treatment: people receive the same treatment, no matter who they are or what they believe.

Equal opportunity: Everyone has the same chance as everyone else to receive an education or promotion at work. Opportunities are open to people based on their abilities and factors such as gender, race, disability, religious belief, sexual orientation or age should not lead to someone receiving unfair treatment.

Wordbox

DISCRIMINATION
This means to be treated in a less favourable way than other people. It includes the workplace, at school or having access to important services, such as healthcare.

Unlawful Discrimination

It is against the law for an employer to discriminate against someone because of their gender, race, disability, religious belief, sexual orientation or age. The law recognises that discrimination is not simply unfairness. To be discriminated against means to be treated in a less favourable way than other people in the same or similar circumstances.

The laws that seek to protect potentially vulnerable groups of people often refer to four types of discrimination:

1. **Direct** – A person is treated less favourably because of gender, race, etc.
2. **Indirect** – An unfair condition or practice is applied which excludes or causes disadvantage to some people or groups of people.
3. **Victimisation** – This means to single someone out for less favourable treatment, perhaps because they have complained about discrimination in the past.
4. **Harassment** – This includes name-calling and spiteful remarks and creating an intimidating or hostile environment for another person.

If a person is treated in any of these ways at work, or when they are applying for a job, then they may be facing discrimination and there are laws in place to protect them.

There are separate laws in Northern Ireland for each of these different areas:

- **Gender**
- **Race**
- **Disability**
- **Religious belief**
- **Sexual orientation**
- **Age**

DISCUSSION
Can you think of any other groups of people that might face discrimination in the workplace?

43

There are also specific regulations for the workplace. The following looks in more detail at the equality laws relating to gender, race and disability and how they affect employers and employees.

Gender

Sex discrimination includes unfavourable treatment on the basis of:

- Gender
- Marital status
- Pregnancy

The Sex Discrimination laws protect a person whether they are already employed or an applicant for a job. For example, an employer could not turn down a married man for a job on the grounds that family commitments might get in the way of his work and employ a single person instead. A promotion in the workplace must also be equally available to both male and female applicants. If the best person was pregnant and about to start maternity leave, an employer would still have to offer the promotion, to commence when she returned to work. An employer should also ensure that a worker who is in the process of changing gender is not harassed by other staff.

The Sexual Discrimination Order (Northern Ireland) 1976 makes sure that an employer cannot treat a person less favourably because of their sex. **The Equal Pay Act (Northern Ireland) 1970** requires that men and women are paid the same for doing the same or similar work.

However, there are some cases where a job can be advertised for someone of a particular sex. This is where there is a 'genuine occupational requirement'. Here are some examples:

- Some jobs in single-sex schools.
- Jobs involving physical contact where a person could object to being treated by someone of the opposite sex.
- Acting jobs that need a man or woman.

CASE STUDY: HOW I DEALT WITH DISCRIMINATION

Kirsty, 25, was becoming depressed following a stream of sexist harassment from her male colleagues. Finally she took control of the situation though, and proved that their behaviour was unacceptable.

"I had always dreamed of a high flying city career so when I graduated I worked hard to get a job in a well respected financial institution. I knew I had the skills to do well and was really excited to get started.

The other men in my group were hostile to me from the moment that I started. I found out later that I had taken a role that they thought was going to one of their friends so I think they resented me.

To begin with they did not make any sexist comments but were just generally cold and unhelpful. I naively thought that I just had to prove myself and their attitudes towards me would turn around."

Unfortunately, things soon went from bad to worse for Kirsty, and however hard she worked, she couldn't break through.

"It started in a subtle way to begin with, with the odd comment here and there. I thought I was just being sensitive and put up with it. However, soon my male colleagues were making overtly sexual jokes around me and insinuating things that made me feel very uncomfortable.

It was past the point of making a joke of it so I tried to talk to the ringleader and ask why he was being like that. He played innocent and apologised for any 'misinterpretation' but nothing changed. In fact, I think he just wound up his friends more and the harassment became more frequent.

Their behaviour was getting to me so much that I dreaded going into work and slipped into a spate of depression. I knew I couldn't let them win so I finally plucked up the courage to do something about it. I started keeping notes of everything they said and did so that I had a good record.

Then I made an appointment and approached my boss about it. I expected him to be unsympathetic but actually he took my complaint very seriously. The grievance was dealt with in-house and the men received disciplinary action and were moved to different departments.

It felt great that somebody was on my side and that I had stood up for myself. Since then I have been treated as an equal by my new colleagues and am happy and thriving in my role. I would advise anyone who is being discriminated against to find the courage to speak up. It's not your fault, it shouldn't be tolerated and you can get back your life and your confidence back."

Reproduced courtesy of www.AboutEqualOpportunities.co.uk

Story taken from http://www.aboutequalopportunities.co.uk/dealing-with-discrimination-case-study.html

KEY QUESTION

How did Kirsty deal with the discrimination she faced at work?

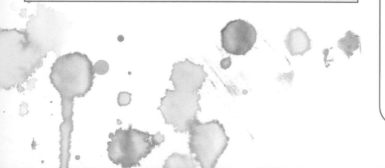

Race

It is unlawful for an employer to discriminate on racial grounds. These include:

- Race
- Colour
- Nationality
- Ethnic or national origins

The laws against discrimination at work cover every part of employment, including recruitment, terms and conditions of employment, pay, training and promotion. For example, a person could not be refused a job simply because an employer felt their ethnic background might cause problems with other employees. If an employer asked for a higher level of English speaking than a job needed, this could be indirect discrimination as it excludes certain people. If someone is subjected to remarks about their colour or nationality in the workplace, this can also be discrimination and it is unlawful.

The Race Relations Order (Northern Ireland) 1997 protects all racial groups in the workplace. Irish Travellers have special protection under this law as they are defined as a racial group.

THE EQUALITY COMMISSION FOR NORTHERN IRELAND

The Equality Commission works to promote equality of opportunity and good relations in Northern Ireland. It is an independent public body. The Commission is responsible for helping employers to understand the law. It advises employers on policies and practices that will help ensure they do not discriminate. Discrimination is not always deliberate but the law allows people to complain even if the employer did not mean to discriminate.

How the Equality Commission helps employers

The Equality Commission provides advice and training to employers who need to know the law on discrimination. The Commission runs general awareness campaigns to help employers be aware of racism, sectarianism and other forms of discrimination in the workplace. Many campaigns are organised in partnership with trade unions and other groups who are also working to ensure greater equality in society. As discrimination law changes, the Commission will ensure that employers know about the changes and what they must do to avoid complaints of discrimination.

There are many advisory publications on the Commission's website which give employers guidance on how to ensure equality of opportunity. The Commission produces Codes of practice. If an employer does not follow the guidance in a Code, this may mean that an employee who takes a complaint of discrimination will win their case.

Employability and positive action

In some cases the law allows employers to take particular steps to recruit unemployed people and to help other disadvantaged groups to get a job. For example, employers may be able to target some jobs at people who are long-term unemployed even if there are other people who would be able to do the job. Employers are able to take special steps to make sure that women or men know they can apply for jobs that are usually done by the opposite sex. This is called 'positive action'. They still have to have a fair procedure for selecting who gets the job, however. Positive action is designed to ensure greater equality for groups that suffer a particular disadvantage.

How the Equality Commission helps employees

The Commission provides advice and support to people who think they have been discriminated against at work. Help ranges from helping people to sort out a problem with their employer to advising them about how to bring a formal complaint to an industrial tribunal.

Information from http://www.equalityni.org

The Equality Commission welcomes requests for further information from students, teachers and members of the public.

Phone 02890 890 890 or visit their website: www.equalityni.org

RESEARCH ACTIVITY

Use the Internet to find out what other organisations offer advice to employers and employees on discrimination in the workplace.

Disability

Having a disability might include:

- Vision impairment, such as partial sight or blindness.
- Reduced mobility, perhaps using a wheelchair.
- A hearing impairment.
- A mental disability.

Disabled workers have the same rights as anyone else, but they have additional rights under the **Disability Discrimination Act 1995**. This law protects people from discrimination if they have a disability which is long-term and affects their ability to do day-to-day activities. People who have been diagnosed with cancer, HIV or Multiple Sclerosis (MS) are automatically defined as having a disability.

It is unlawful for an employer to treat a disabled person less favourably than another person. The law covers all aspects of employment, including:

- Application forms
- Arrangements for interview
- Job offers
- Terms of employment
- Promotion and training
- Access to refreshment or toilet facilities

An employer has a legal obligation to make 'reasonable adjustments' to the workplace and to job duties so that a disabled employee is not put at a disadvantage compared to non-disabled workers. This may include specially adapted equipment, such as a computer or desk, and accessible washroom facilities. A workplace may have written instructions or posters displaying health and safety information. An employer may have to consider how to make these accessible for a person with impaired vision, for example. An employer will probably need to discuss any adjustments with the disabled worker. Both will need to consider how effective something is likely to be and whether it is likely to cause any disruption.

An employer must not deny training opportunities to an employee who is disabled, but must make reasonable arrangements to improve the accessibility of a training programme, by choosing a different location if necessary. This responsibility might involve producing an audio or Braille version of training manuals and a sign language interpreter being made available at training sessions.

CASE STUDY: COPING WITH MY CAREER AND A DISABILITY

Alex, 42, has been in a wheelchair since he was 7. He says that most of his experiences at work have been good, although some companies still have a long way to go.

"I have been in wheelchair for most of my life and attended a mainstream school so I have never thought of myself as different or even disabled. Yes, some things are a little harder for me, but with a little bit of thought and some adaptations I can manage to do most things an able-bodied person could.

When I left school I started working in IT. My first employer was very forward thinking for the time and made a great effort to make sure that all my needs were met and that I wasn't treated any differently from any other employee. I am very glad that they were my first experience of the workplace as it allowed me to see what is possible.

When I was in my late 20s I was looking for a bit of a change and got a job as an IT training manager in a small company. As soon as I started though, I realised that it was a mistake. I think they took me on because they needed to show they had filled their quota of disabled people rather than actually wanting me there.

Nothing was set up conveniently for me and it was a constant challenge to get things changed. I also found myself excluded from certain meetings because access for the wheelchair was impossible and had decisions made over my head. Eventually I took them to an employment tribunal and won, which was a good boost to my confidence."

Alex says that he is happy that discrimination is now taken seriously but people's attitudes need to change if disabled people are going to be treated equally.

"Apart from that one company I have always been treated well by my employers but you still have to face some ignorance from colleagues. I think all companies need to offer training about dealing with disability and help promote understanding and acceptance in the workplace.

That is what I do now. I have set up my own company which I never dreamed of when I was younger. Companies all across the country bring me and my team in to run training sessions and it is very satisfying. Attitudes have definitely changed and as the younger generation come into the workplace I think it will only get better.

No disabled person should ever feel that they have to settle for sub-standard facilities or unfair treatment. If they are capable of doing the job as well as their colleagues then they should be given the same opportunities.

Legislations have definitely helped but I think that individuals also need to take responsibility for their own treatment. If you feel that you are being discriminated against then don't be afraid to speak up. Employers must be accountable for their actions and you need to make sure that you are judged by your ability not your disability."

Story taken from http://www.aboutequalopportunities. co.uk/coping-with-career-disability-case-study.html

KEY QUESTION

How did Alex deal with the discrimination he faced at work?

CHECK YOUR LEARNING

1. What is discrimination?
2. Explain how people are protected from discrimination at work, on the grounds of gender, race and disability.

EXTENSION TASK

Choose one of the types of discrimination in the workplace covered in this chapter.

Produce a PowerPoint presentation on this topic that could be presented to the rest of the class.

evaluation

Evaluate the effectiveness of the law in protecting individuals from discrimination in the workplace.

Health and safety

Health and safety is all about reducing the risk of an injury or preventing people from becoming ill through their work. Health and safety is the responsibility of everyone in the workplace but it is the employer who has a legal duty to make sure the Health and safety laws are kept.

The Health and Safety at Work (Northern Ireland) Order 1978 is the main legislation which applies to all workplaces in Northern Ireland. There are other laws which apply to specific occupations, such as safe use of chemicals or pesticides. The **Health and Safety Executive for Northern Ireland** is responsible making sure these regulations are carried out and can inspect places of work.

Under this legislation, employers must decide what could potentially injure an employee or lead to ill health, as a result of their work. This is known as a **risk assessment**. The employer then has to take measures to control these risks. For example, a noisy piece of machinery might cause damage to hearing. The employer has a regulation for the workplace that all employees using this machinery must wear the special ear protection, which is provided. A risk assessment is important because it helps an employer to focus on what are the health and safety issues in their workplace. The law does not expect employers to eliminate all risks, but to protect their employers as far as possible. As part of these obligations, employers must also make sure that all staff are trained in health and safety procedures, know where to receive first aid treatment and are clear about what to do in an emergency.

ACTIVITY

Use a computer to design a leaflet suitable for new employees.

- In your leaflet, outline the responsibilities of the employer and employee with regard to health and safety issues.
- You will need to decide what workplace or business your leaflet is designed for.

Work-related stress is becoming increasingly common in recent years. One in five people suffers from workplace stress, with half a million people reporting that they have become ill as a result.*

To a certain extent, it can be good to feel under some pressure as it means you are being challenged. It can also motivate a person to get on with a particular task and have the satisfaction of achieving results. However, if this pressure is excessive and causes a person to feel unwell, then it has become stress and is a potentially serious health concern. Some common causes of work-related stress include poor communication, a poor working environment, and employees doing a job for which they have not had proper training. Stress may also be caused by bullying in the workplace, perhaps because of a person's race or disability. The anti-discrimination laws which have already been described are there to protect a person in this situation. If a person has a disability and suffers stress because workplace conditions are difficult for them, an employer has a duty to make adjustments to try and help.

* Statistics taken from http://www.direct.gov.uk/en/Employment/HealthAndSafetyAtWork/DG_10026604

CASE STUDY: FEELING WELL, DOING WELL IN THE PSNI

The Police Service of Northern Ireland employs approximately 7,500 officers and 2,700 administrative employees.

At the start of 2009, the PSNI decided to dramatically improve the health and well-being of their employees and launched a campaign 'Feeling Well, Doing Well'. A key part of this initiative was providing employees with access to the well-being hub (an online support system designed to boost employee health and well-being).

Through logging into the well-being hub, PSNI employees can access advice on a wide range of health and well-being topics including healthy eating, work-life balance and relaxation techniques. The PSNI can also communicate to their employees on well-being policies and keep them up to date with new initiatives. For example, the 'Cycle to Work' initiative attracted over 20% of the workforce to register.

As a result of their well-being scheme, the PSNI has dramatically improved health support throughout the workforce.

Information taken from http://www.thewellbeinghub.com/pdf/Case-PSNI.pdf

AREAS OF RESPONSIBILITY TOWARDS AN EMPLOYEE

There are some basic work rights that everyone is entitled to, from their first day of work. These are:

- National Minimum Wage
- Working time rights (such as breaks, holidays and a limit on the number of hours in a working week)
- Health and safety protection
- The right to join a trade union
- Protection from unlawful discrimination

Contract of employment

An employer has a number of areas of responsibility towards an employee. Some of these are contained in the contract of employment while others come from laws passed by the government. A contract of employment is an agreement between the employer and employee. This contract is made as soon as a person accepts a job and an employee is entitled to a written contract within two months of starting work. The contract will set out important details, for example:

- The starting date of the employment and whether the work is temporary or permanent
- Salary
- Hours of work, holiday pay and entitlement to sick pay
- Where the employee will be working
- Period of notice needed to end the employment
- Information on pension schemes
- Information on disciplinary and grievance procedures

The details which are written down are called the express terms of a contract. There are also implied terms of a contract where an employer is expected to have a duty of care towards an employee. An important element implied in a contract of employment is the idea of mutual trust and confidence. The employer and employee both have to be able to trust each other.

ACTIVITY

Construct a spider diagram to show the reasons why it is important for an employee to be given a contract of employment for a job.

Salary

Nearly all workers aged 16 years of age and older are entitled to minimum pay, although different rates apply until a person reaches 21 years of age. The contract of employment will give exact information about the rate of pay, but it should not be below the National Minimum Wage, or at odds with the Equal Pay Act. Whether salary will be paid weekly or monthly should also be covered by the contract. Employees must be told in their written contract what arrangements are made for sick pay. By law, an employee can receive up to 28 weeks Statutory Sick Pay (SSP) through the national insurance contributions scheme.

RESEARCH ACTIVITY

Use the Internet to find out the National Minimum Wage in the UK for each of the following groups:

- Individuals aged 16–17
- Individuals aged 18-20
- Individuals aged 21 and over
- Apprentices under 19 or in their first year of apprenticeship

Holidays

These will be detailed in the contract. Most adult workers are entitled to a minimum of 5.6 weeks annual leave. In addition to this, the law allows for time off to perform public duties. These include jury service, local councillors attending council meetings and members of a school's board of governors attending school committee meetings. Employers do not need to pay employees for time off to carry out these duties, unless it is included in the contract. Weekly working hours and time off during the day will also be covered by the contract of employment. The law states that the maximum length of an average working week should be 48 hours. A person has the right to a break of at least 20 minutes if their working day is more than 6 hours long.

Exceptional circumstances

If an employee has suffered a bereavement of a close family member, then it is expected that they should have three days compassionate leave. This may not be written into a contract of employment, but it is an area where an employer is expected to show a duty of care towards an employee. It is also expected that a worker with dependants could take a reasonable amount of time off to deal with a family emergency, such as a child being taken into hospital.

Career development

This is another area where an employer has a duty of care towards an employee. It is widely accepted that lifelong learning is crucial and an employer should not stop staff from having access to training. However, good employers will go beyond the basic requirements and give their employees plenty of opportunities to learn new skills and develop their career. This could be through training sessions held in the workplace or by making sure that employees have the opportunity to go to organised classes outside work.

The role of Trade Unions

A trade Union represents the rights of employees in the workplace, ensuring that employers meet their legal obligations and responsibilities. These might include working hours, pay or health and safety issues. If someone makes a formal complaint against a person in the context of their job, then a trade union will represent the employee, in court if necessary. There are different trade unions for different professions. A teacher, for example, will be a member of a different union than an engineering worker or a nurse. Trade unions specialise in the issues that effect workers in a particular occupation.

There are also disadvantages to Trade unions. Powerful Trade Unions can bargain for high wages. If wages are forced to be too high then this can cause unemployment and a rise in inflation. If a Trade Union calls for strike action, a company could lose money and go out of business. This could result in redundancies. Trade Unions are there to represent workers, but they also cost employees money. An annual fee has to be paid to the union, but a worker who chooses not to go on strike and crosses a picket line may be fined by their union.

WHAT IS A TRADE UNION?

A trade union is an organisation made up of members (a membership-based organisation) and its membership must be made up mainly of workers. One of a trade union's main aims is to protect and advance the interests of its members in the workplace.

Most trade unions are independent of any employer. However, trade unions try to develop close working relationships with employers. This can sometimes take the form of a partnership agreement between the employer and the trade union which identifies their common interests and objectives.

Trade unions:

- negotiate agreements with employers on pay and conditions.
- discuss major changes to the workplace such as large scale redundancy.
- discuss their members' concerns with employers.
- accompany their members in disciplinary and grievance meetings.
- provide their members with legal and financial advice.
- provide education facilities and certain consumer benefits such as discounted insurance.

Information from http://www.direct.gov.uk/en/Employment/TradeUnions/Tradeunionmembership/DG_10027544

INVESTORS IN PEOPLE

This is an award for organisations of all sizes and in all areas of employment. Investors in People was set up in 1991 and became the responsibility of the UK Commission for employment and skills in April 2010. The aim of the award is for organisations to meet high standards in the way they manage their employees and help them develop in their career. An improvement in people management leads to a more efficient business and better public services.

CHARTER MARK

The Charter Mark standard helps organisations to improve customer service, by putting customers first and giving value for money. Once the standard is awarded, organisations are assessed once a year to make sure they still meet the standard. There are a number of goals that have to be met and there is emphasis on good relations with staff as well as customers.

CHECK YOUR LEARNING

1. Name the Health and Safety Legislation that applies to the workplace.
2. Under the Health and Safety Legislation, what are the responsibilities of employers and employees?
3. What is a contract of employment and why is it important for both an employer and employee?
4. What is a Trade Union?
5. Explain how an employee can benefit from being a member of a Trade Union.

THE RESPONSIBILITIES OF AN EMPLOYEE

Rights and responsibilities in the workplace are a two-way process. An employee has rights that must be met. In return, an employee also has responsibilities towards their employer and other workers. Some of the responsibilities an employee has will be outlined in their contract and these must be kept. However, the law also says that an employee has certain duties and obligations even if they are not mentioned in their contract.

What can an employer expect from an employee?

- **Loyalty** – Employees should not pass on any confidential information about their employer. Employees also have a duty not to compete in business against their employer while working for them as an employee. If an employee has to use the employer's property, then they should look after it properly.

- **Honesty –** Employees have a duty to be honest. This includes not telling lies or withholding information (such as time spent in prison) in your application, not taking bribes related to your work and not stealing from your employer. Taking goods or materials home from work, unless you have permission to do so, counts as stealing from your employer.

- **Reliability** – Time keeping is an important issue. Even the most conscientious worker can face a transport problem occasionally, but an employee should not be continually late for work or taking longer breaks than necessary. If your employer often has to find people to cover for you because of your unpunctuality, you are not likely to be a good investment! Employees are entitled to time off work if unwell, but this should not be abused. Employees are expected not to take time off sick unless they are genuinely too ill for work.

- **Meeting deadlines –** Employees should work to the best of their ability and try to have a positive attitude to work. Employers like workers to have a good work ethic and do their best to complete tasks and within a realistic time frame. An employee who makes little effort to meet deadlines could lead to their employer losing business.

DISCUSSION

Do you have a part-time job? If so, do you think you show these qualities at work?

Health and Safety

Health and safety in the workplace is the responsibility of everyone. An employer has a legal duty to meet the necessary regulations, but all employees have responsibilities, too. Some of these are:

- To take care with your own health and safety.
- To take care not to put other employees or members of the public at risk through your behaviour.
- To co-operate with your employer and make sure you follow the health and safety policies for your workplace.
- To tell your employer if there is a medical reason why you may not be able to do your job properly, especially if you drive or operate machinery as part of your work.
- Not to misuse any equipment that has been provided to keep people safe.

evaluation

Evaluate the impact of Health and Safety Legislation in the workplace.

THE CONSEQUENCES OF NOT MEETING RESPONSIBILITIES

It is important for an employee to have a contract so that both the employer and the employee have legal protection if the contract is not kept. If an employee breaks their contract, their employer should first of all try and settle the matter informally. However, they are entitled to sue for damages, the same way an employee can sue them. Damages are only awarded if an employee causes their employer to loose money. For example, if person ends their employment but leaves without giving enough notice, the employer may have to hire temporary staff until the post can be filled. This is one of the most common ways in which employees break their contract.

For any other breaches of contract, a person's job may be at risk. This may also be the case if an employee causes an accident through deliberately ignoring health and safety advice.

If an employee is simply lazy, a poor timekeeper or generally unenthusiastic about their work then the consequence may be that they are not considered for promotion and cannot progress in their career.

REWARDS AND BONUSES

Rewards and bonus schemes are becoming popular with employers as a way to motivate employees and encourage hard work.

- **Commission** – With this scheme, a person is paid according to how productive they are in their work. A person whose job is to sell something – a fitted kitchen or foreign holiday, for example, will be paid according to their sales. A similar idea is piece rate, where a person's job is to make something and they are paid a set rate for each item they produce. With piece rate and commission, employees who make an extra effort are rewarded for it and are more likely to feel appreciated. However, some employees may worry about losing pay if there is a drop in sales, or if their work rate is affected by other employees.

- **Profit-sharing** – With this arrangement, an employee's pay is linked directly to the profits of the business they are working for. This incentive works best in businesses where profit is the main focus. Recent surveys suggest that around two thirds of UK companies have some sort of profit-sharing scheme. Some businesses reward their employees with a share in the profits by giving shares in the company.

- **Non-financial incentives** – On the spot rewards for good work are becoming increasingly popular. These instant rewards can help to motivate staff and make them feel appreciated, encouraging more positive behaviour in the future. A 'thank you' gift for an employee could be a box of chocolates, a gift voucher or perhaps an experience day. Other incentives offered by employers include lunch vouchers and discounts on products.

ACTIVITY

Produce a questionnaire and interview members of your family who are in employment.

- How do they rate their employer?
- Do they feel their employer could do more to reward and motivate good employees?
- If so, why is this?

to
the
in their
law also s
obligations e
contract.

52

QUIZ: HAS THE LAW BEEN BROKEN?

Use your knowledge of the legislation covered by this chapter to decide if the law has been broken in each of these situations.

1. A disabled employee cannot use the canteen as there is no wheelchair access. He does, however, have access to the vending machines.

2. A new employee has still not been given a written contract of employment by the end of his second week at work.

3. A woman is turned down for a promotion because she is pregnant and about to start her maternity leave.

4. An employee did not mention on his application form that in the past he had a short prison sentence. He lied about dates to cover this up.

5. Health and safety advice is clearly displayed on posters around the workplace. However, this advice is not available in any other format for visually impaired employees.

6. An employee from an ethnic minority group is paid less than other workers, on the grounds that her spoken English is not fluent. However, this does not prevent her from carrying out her job as well as anyone else.

7. A job advertisement for a nurse states that the applicant must be a woman. The position is for a residential post in an all-girls boarding school.

8. An employee leaves without working the period of notice given in his contract.

9. An employee has to do jury service. Her employer is happy to give time off from work, but without pay.

10. An employee knows he must wear ear protection when using the floor polishing machine, but most of the time he does not bother.

1. YES – Disabled employees must have access to adequate refreshment and washroom facilities, the same as any other worker.
2. NO – Employers have up to two months to issue a written contract.
3. YES – This is an example of discrimination on the grounds of gender.
4. YES – It is unlawful to lie on an application form. A person could lose their job as a result.
5. YES – Employers must make sure Health and safety advice is available to all employees. An audio presentation or Braille should also be available.
6. YES – This is an example of discrimination on the grounds of race.
7. NO – In certain situations, a job can be advertised specifically for men or women.
8. YES – The written contract of employment is a legally binding document. The employer could seek damages through the courts if the former employee has caused him to lose money.
9. NO – An employer must let an employee off work, but does not have to offer any pay. The employee has to claim for loss of earnings through the courts.
10. YES – All employees have a duty to follow Health and safety legislation. An employee who refuses to use safety equipment could lose his job.

THE NEED FOR SOCIAL AWARENESS

What is 'Social Awareness'? Any business, large or small, is going to have an interest in making a profit. However, there is growing concern that businesses should act in a responsible way. This means making decisions which show responsibility for the environment and towards the local community in which they work. It can also involve thinking about where raw materials come from: have they been produced in a way which does not exploit people or cause unnecessary cruelty to animals? If a business becomes more socially aware then everyone can benefit – including the business itself.

ENVIRONMENTAL ISSUES

Showing concern for the environment is everyone's responsibility, from the child who drops a crisp packet to the multi-national company with the potential to cause widespread pollution. However, there are some environmental issues of particular concern to businesses and a range of positive action that they can take to show social awareness.

Waste

All businesses produce waste – from the office producing waste paper and empty ink cartridges to the factory with chemical waste to be dealt with. There are many ways in which businesses can take positive action to deal with the problem of waste, for example, by **reducing, reusing** and **recycling**. There are also financial benefits for businesses that reduce their waste, as less waste means less landfill tax to pay.

All businesses must ensure that their waste is contained properly, so it does not leak or blow away, and an authorised company must also collect it for disposal. **Litter** can be an important issue for some businesses, particularly fast food outlets, and responsible retailers will provide adequate bins for food wrappings. There are laws in place to make sure that dangerous or poisonous waste is dealt with correctly and businesses can be fined heavily for ignoring these regulations.

RESEARCH ACTIVITY

Work in a groups of 4 for this activity.

- Choose a local business in your area.
- Find out about the work they do and how they operate.
- Suggest ways in which you think this business could reduce, reuse and recycle.
- Research what this business is actually doing about the problem of waste.

Climate change

Climate change is a serious global problem and even small businesses can have an impact. There is concern that greenhouse gases are causing a worldwide increase in heat waves, floods and droughts. Most of the energy used in the UK comes from fossil fuels, such as coal, oil or gas. These sources of energy are considered to be making a significant contribution to the problem of greenhouse gases.

A responsible business could consider the following:

- **Transport** – How do employees travel to work? What use is made of company cars? Do delivery vehicles operate efficiently?
- **Energy consumption** – What sources of energy are used in buildings and for manufacturing? Are there ways to be more efficient? Could alternative sources of energy be used?
- **Renewable energy** – A business could investigate using a source of renewable energy, such as solar, wind or wave power, which could save money and reduce the amount of greenhouse gases that are produced. At present, this option is more likely to be practical for a business that can afford to make a substantial

investment. However, smaller organisations could still try to be energy efficient.

Energy efficiency

Saving energy can save money for a business. There will be reduced bills if employees are encouraged to be careful, for example, by turning off lights at the end of the day. Businesses can also save money by making changes to the work area, so less energy is used, for example:

- **Lighting** – installing skylights in an office could increase natural light and mean that less electricity is used.

- **Heat** – better insulation for buildings could help to provide a pleasant working temperature without the need for excessive heating or air conditioning.

- **Equipment** – replacing old equipment with a more energy efficient model could save money in the long-term.

Businesses may also attract customers by showing that they are environmentally friendly. It is not currently a legal requirement for businesses to save energy, but the government has introduced incentives to encourage businesses to be energy efficient.

CYCLE TO WORK SCHEME

Cycle to Work is a government initiative designed to help employees buy a new bike to commute to work, once their employer has signed up with the scheme. The idea is to promote healthier journeys to work and reduce environmental pollution. Many different places of employment are now part of this scheme as a way of showing environmental awareness and a concern for the well-being of employees.

CASE STUDY: McDONALDS

McDonald's 26 restaurants in Northern Ireland are committed to supporting the local community through their involvement in local initiatives and protecting the local area.

McDonald's mission is: *"To be the UK's best family restaurant and we believe that this involves protecting the environment at the local and global level. We strive to ensure that our operations today do not have a negative impact on the lives of future generations."*

McDonald's base its environmental programme on 'reduce, reuse and recycle'. Here are some of the ways they are doing this:

- Energy efficiency is being improved in restaurants.

- Daily litter patrols try to keep the area around restaurants litter-free.

- Restaurants participate in Tidy NI's Big Spring Clean Campaign.

- McDonald's has a voluntary programme in place inviting staff to become Planet Champions and act as the environmental voice in the restaurant, helping business managers with existing environment initiatives and generating new ideas.

- Cardboard packaging is made of 72% recycled paper.

- Bags and napkins contain 100% recycled materials.

- Solid waste is disposed of responsibly.

- Drainage systems are being installed to combat grease and improve the quality of waste water.

- McDonald's is working with The Carbon Trust to try and reduce its carbon footprint. For example, an alarm sounds on a burger grill that has not been used for a period of time, reminding employees to turn it to standby mode to save energy.

Information taken from http://www.mcdonalds.co.uk/ourworld/environment/policy.shtml

RESEARCH ACTIVITY

Choose another multi-national company or a small local business.

- What are they doing to show social responsibility or concern for the environment?

- You could use the Internet for research or make contact with a local business (perhaps through email).

There is plenty of advice available to help businesses act responsibly, keep within the law and save money!

Some useful websites:

- Business in the Community – www.bitc.org.uk/northern_ireland/index.html

- Carbon Trust – www.carbontrust.co.uk

- NetRegs – www.netregs.gov.uk

- nibusinessinfo.co.uk – www.nibusinessinfo.co.uk

- Northern Ireland Environment Agency – www.doeni.gov.uk/niea/business_and_industry-2.htm

NEWS ITEM

ONLINE RESOURCE OFFERS HELP WITH 'GREEN' BUSINESS REGULATIONS

A new website aimed at helping small businesses in Northern Ireland understand the environmental legislation affecting their work has been launched.

NetRegs – www.netregs.gov.uk – offers general advice on environmental issues such as waste, storage of materials and water and energy efficiencies, as well as information on forthcoming legislation and good practice advice that can help businesses save money.

Commenting on the site, Richard Rogers, Chief Executive of DOE's Environment & Heritage Service said: "We recognise that many smaller businesses have limited time and resources to keep on top of their environmental obligations and that is why we have set up the NetRegs website, to give them the help they need to protect both the environment and their business."

It is estimated that smaller businesses in the UK generate about 60% of commercial waste and are responsible for as much as 80% of pollution incidents.

The NetRegs website, developed by EHS in partnership with the UK's other environmental regulators, also provides guidance on the environmental regulations governing 50 industry sectors.

Source: 'Online resource offers help with 'green' business regulations', 4ni.co.uk, 13 May 2004, http://www.4ni.co.uk/northern_ireland_news

SUSTAINABILITY

A sustainable business is a 'green business'. This means it does not have a negative impact on the environment, either locally or globally. The methods used in production and the end product will be environmentally friendly. A sustainable business will trade responsibly and show a concern for the community in which it operates.

Sustainable sources

Every product that a business buys will have an impact on the environment, whether it is paper for the printer or new farm machinery. Businesses could be 'greener' by buying goods that have come from a sustainable source, and choosing suppliers that use less packaging and create less waste. They could show social awareness by using goods that have been produced locally, which will cut down on the fuel needed for transport, reduce emissions and help to boost the local economy. If businesses do buy from overseas, they could make sure that the products they buy have been fairly traded and do not involve exploitation of people in the developing world. Similarly, Catering businesses, such as restaurants, could show social awareness by making a point of using free range eggs and meat from animals that have been reared in humane conditions.

Inner city renewal and development

In recent years, the government has made neighbourhood renewal a priority, with many new development schemes. Deprived inner city areas are being developed and a successful mix of housing, leisure, business and services has been achieved. For example, disused factories have been replaced with shopping centres, derelict areas become parkland and old docks are now home to restaurants and cinemas. These initiatives have created new jobs and also led to changes in employment, as traditional occupations are replaced with new ones.

Sometimes inner city renewal can be unpopular. New supermarkets and large stores are often part of the development package, and there is concern that small shops cannot cope with the competition. Local family businesses are then forced to close. Some people are also concerned that new housing in these areas often consists of apartments for professional people, rather than family homes.

Today, new projects are often discussed with local residents so that agreement can be reached about what is best for the local community. In Northern Ireland, a number of areas have been targeted for development by the Department for Social Development. The case study below gives a success story.

CASE STUDY: *Examples of Urban Development Grant projects*

WINTERTHURLIFE UK LTD, HOLYWOOD ROAD, BELFAST

This scheme involved the demolition of a derelict library building that had been vacant since 1992 and the construction of a 5-storey office building for owner occupation. This scheme gave a leverage of 5.89 (i.e. for every £1 of public money spent on this project, £5.89 of private monies was also spent). This scheme also contributed 500m^2 of commercial floor space and created an additional 10 new jobs.

Information from http://www.dsdni.gov.uk/udg

HOW COULD IT BENEFIT A BUSINESS TO SHOW SOCIAL AWARENESS?

In short, it can be good for business, good for the environment and good for the community! Here are some examples:

Corporate Image

Having a social awareness may attract more customers and increase profit for the business. For example, a supermarket that makes an effort to have a range of fairly traded products may appeal to customers who like to shop responsibly. Businesses can enhance their corporate image by showing a concern for the environment and the wider world.

A more productive workforce

A person may be unhappy working for an organisation if they do not approve of their business practices. However, if they share the same values as the business, they are more likely to show loyalty to their employer. Some prospective employees may be attracted to businesses that show social awareness. As a result, they may contribute to a more productive workforce.

Costs are lowered

Environmental initiatives such as recycling could work out cheaper for the business, therefore saving them money. Some employers now offer incentives to employees to be environmentally friendly at work. A worker who is wasteful with resources is not helping the environment and costing their employer money. Buying locally produced raw materials, where possible, is more sustainable and could save on transport costs for a business.

Carbon footprint

A modern business could show responsibility by having an awareness of their carbon footprint. This means taking a careful assessment of all the greenhouse gases that are produced from business activities and investigating ways to try and reduce them. If a business can reduce its energy consumption, or switch to a renewable source, then this is better for the environment and may save the business money.

Wordbox

Carbon footprint
A Carbon footprint is the measure of the amount of carbon dioxide produced by a person or business and the environmental impact of these emissions.

Business ethics

There is a growing interest in business ethics. Many people are placing increasing importance on businesses acting responsibly towards employees, the community and the environment. Realising this, some businesses are showing an awareness of global issues and the long term advantage of putting people before profits.

ACTIVITY

Choose two of the following businesses and draw a spider diagram for each, giving examples of how each one might show social awareness.

- A takeaway food outlet
- A family business made up of a farm and a butchers shop
- An architect's office
- A day care nursery
- A hairdressing salon

Your teacher might ask you to complete this activity in a group and produce your diagram on a page from a flip chart (or something similar). You could be asked to explain your ideas to the rest of the class.

1. How can businesses show:

   a) An awareness of environmental issues?
   b) Sustainability?
   c) Social responsibility?

2. How can it benefit a business to show social and environmental concern?

ACTIVITY

ROLE PLAY

Work in groups of about 6 for this, with each person in the group taking on one of the roles below. Role play the meeting, with each person taking a turn to present their view.

THE NEW SHOPPING CENTRE

Background

A small town is to be the focus of a new development. A large supermarket is keen to open one of its stores there and it is to be the main retailer in a new shopping centre. The supermarket and shopping centre will bring jobs to the area and a greater choice of products available locally to residents. However, a row of old cottages will have to be demolished, as well as a small area of woodland, to build the new shopping centre. Feelings about the project are mixed in the town and a meeting is held in a local community centre to hear people's views.

The people involved

- **Jack McMillan** has owned and run Jackie's Corner Shop for the last thirty years. He is very concerned about the new supermarket, fearing it will force him out of business.

- **Ms Smith** is the Public Relations Officer for the supermarket. It is her job to promote the new venture as much as possible. The last thing she wants is any bad publicity or local people protesting as the building work is about to go ahead.

- **Nancy** is 34 years old and fed up with being stuck at home now her children are in primary school. She would love a part-time job and welcomes the idea of the new centre.

- **George** is 78 years old has lived in the cottages all his life. He does not want to move and thinks a new shopping centre is the last thing the town needs. He is also concerned that local businesses will lose their livelihood.

- **Sandra and Anne** are teenage sisters who think it will be brilliant to have some decent shops locally without having to spend a fortune on bus fares. They are also hoping there might be Saturday jobs available in one of the new shops.

- **Kevin** runs a market garden business, supplying local greengrocers with vegetables and fruit. He has mixed feelings about the new centre. If his local buyers go out of business it will affect him badly; on the other hand the supermarket has promised to buy local produce so the opportunity to sell to them might be very good for his business.

evaluation

Evaluate the impact of urban renewal on local communities.

EXAM FOCUS

In Chapter one, we looked at the skill of clearly **demonstrating your knowledge and understanding.**

The following question will give you further practice at this:

(a)   Give one Health and Safety procedure which the employer could put in place to help protect employees in the workplace.

[1 mark]

(b)   Identify and explain one reason why it is important for an employee to be given a Contract of Employment by their employer.

[2 marks]

(c)   Identify and explain one advantage of an employee being a member of a Trade Union.

[2 marks]

When answering part (b) and part (c) of this question, start by clearly stating what you are going to write about, then give your explanation.

You could answer part (b) in the following way:

"Holidays and time off work – A Contract of Employment sets out in writing what was agreed when the employee was hired. If there is a dispute about this later on, then the contract can be consulted."

Write your own answer for Part (c).

Question © CCEA from CCEA's GCSE Learning for Life and Work Modular Paper, Unit 5: Employability, May 2010, GLW61

Chapter four

ISSUES OF SELF-EMPLOYMENT AND SOURCES OF SUPPORT

CHAPTER SUMMARY

In this chapter you will be studying:

- The characteristics of an entrepreneur.
- The advantages and disadvantages of being self-employed.
- The help and support available for businesses in Northern Ireland.

INTRODUCTION

Could you be the next Richard Branson or Bill Gates? Have you ever had an original idea for a business or product that you think would sell? With the right marketing and financial backing could you make a success of your idea?

Many people dream of running their own business and being their own boss, especially when employment prospects look bleak. However, running your own business is not necessarily an easy alternative to salaried employment and there are many issues that need to be considered.

THE CHARACTERISTICS OF AN ENTREPRENEUR

Some people can be described as **'enterprising'**. This means they are highly motivated, have a strong need for achievement and believe they have the qualities to be successful. An enterprising person is creative, often setting up projects and seeking new opportunities. They are willing to take a calculated risk, rather than 'play safe' and above all, show determination and perseverance even when things do not go well.

If a person with these enterprising qualities goes into business, then the result is likely to be an **'entrepreneur'**.

63

WHAT IS AN 'ENTREPRENEUR'?

An entrepreneur has an idea for a new venture and sees an opportunity which others do not recognise. They are willing to take responsibility for any risks involved and for the final outcome of the enterprise. French in origin, the word 'entrepreneur' is believed to have been first used in 1800 by French economist Jean Baptiste Say. He defined an entrepreneur as "one who undertakes an enterprise, especially a contractor, acting as intermediary between capital and labour." Therefore, an entrepreneur is primarily a business person who is able to spot an opportunity and market it successfully, taking calculated risks along the way.

COULD YOU BE AN ENTREPRENEUR?

These are some of the qualities which could apply to an entrepreneur. Do you recognise yourself in any of them?

- **Self-motivated** – you set your own goals and work to achieve them.
- **Creative and imaginative** – you come up with new ideas.
- **Intuition** – you can make good guesses when necessary.
- **Opportunistic** – you make the most of every opportunity.
- **Self-confidence** – you believe you can do well if you try.
- **Determination** – you keep going even if things do not go well.
- **Persistence** – you stick at things and do not give up easily.
- **Decisive** – you can make a decision and stick to it.
- **Flexibility** – you are not set in a routine.
- **Competitiveness** – you want to do better than your rivals.
- **Enthusiasm** – you really believe in what you are doing.

- **Positive thinking** – you can see the positive side of every situation.
- **Multi tasking** – you are able to cope with a number of projects at once.
- **Proactive** – you make things happen, rather than sit back and wait.
- **Ability to lead** – you can inspire others and pass on your enthusiasm.

Of course, not all successful business entrepreneurs will possess all these qualities, but they will probably

have quite a few of them in common. Many people with these qualities choose not to go into business, perhaps applying them to a salaried career and being highly successful at it. Some enterprising people pursue personal goals, rather than business ones, such as achieving an Olympic gold medal or climbing the world's highest mountains.

CASE STUDY: A LOCAL ENTREPRENEUR

Sam Morrison, owner of the Northern Ireland-based clothes stores Clockwork Orange, is an example of a local entrepreneur. His business has built a reputation for selling designer clothes for young men and women, selling brands such as Replay, Firetrap, Miss Sixty, Ted Baker, Energie, Killah, Adidas, 55DSL and Hilfiger Denim. This sector of the clothing market has become one of the most competitive in recent years. However, Sam Morrison also has other shops targeting a slightly more mainstream market, selling brands such as Henri-Lloyd and Remus Uomo. The Jeanery opened in 2008, specialising in designer jeans. There is also a hire business, called Hire Class, for wedding suits and clothes for formal occasions.

All these different businesses are part of the SVM Textiles group, of which Sam Morrison is managing director.

Clockwork Orange

Clockwork Orange was first established in Ballymena in the autumn of 1998. Selling a mix of fashion from the established denim giants to independent brands, it was an instant hit among Northern Ireland's youth culture. Due to its success, stores opened up in Newry, Enniskillen, Lisburn and Belfast in the following years, and most recently Derry/Londonderry, Coleraine and Belfast International Airport. Each of the eight stores possesses it's own independent identity but strives to maintain the Clockwork Orange philosophy.

Hire Class

Hire Class is the sister company of Clockwork Orange. It established itself in Ballymena in 2005 and opened its flagship store in Lisburn in 2009. It offers a diverse range of stylish suits for all personalities, which are constantly updated to reflect the latest wedding trends. Its friendly staff provide a personal, tailored service and offer their customers high quality suits, attention to detail and new shirts to keep after the event.

Information from:
www.clockwork-orange.net and
www.hireclassni.com

DISCUSSION

Why do you think entrepreneur Sam Morrison has been successful in business?

STARTING YOUR OWN BUSINESS

Why set up in business? Thousands of people start their own business each year. Some do it because they have had a great idea and have spotted a gap in the market, while others like the idea of being their own boss. Another reason is the possibility of making lots of money. Whatever the reasons for starting a business, it is very important to make careful plans and prepare thoroughly.

RESEARCH

After some initial thinking, the next stage is research. There are four 'W's to consider; what, where, who and why.

What

- What is my product or the service I have to offer?
- What is my unique selling point? I need to be able to stand out from my competitors, so how will I be able to do this?

Where

- Where will my business be located? Will I work from home or have business premises? Are there any competitors located nearby?
- Where will I do business with my customers? Will they come to me, will I need to go to their home, or will everything be completed online?

Who

- Who is the target group for my product? Will everyone want to buy it or is it just for young people, keen gardeners or cyclists, for example?
- Who will run the business? Will I need to do everything myself? Do I have the necessary skills? How will I manage to have time away from the business?

Why

- Why do I want to go into business? Is it just a passing idea or am I really committed to the idea?
- Why will people want to buy what I have to offer? Have I made sure that there is a large enough market for this product or service?

DESIGN

Careful thought needs to be given to the design of the product or service. It is important to have something that will have an impact and is instantly appealing to potential customers. If you plan to market an item, then the design will include the physical appearance of the product, such as shape, colour and the materials it is made from. Then thought will need to be given to features and functions. Is this to be a basic, low cost item or will it be very high tech with plenty of gadgets?

A basic, cheaply priced toaster will probably be available in white plastic and toast bread. A more up-market toaster might come in a variety of colours or chrome, and perhaps even have an extra attachment for toasting bagels and croissants.

An item might be targeted for use with young children, such as a travel cot or playpen. Careful thought needs to be given to the construction and materials used. Is it robust and washable? Are all the materials non-toxic? Some items for children are designed to have a visual impact that will appeal to them. Many of the breakfast cereals targeted at children have brightly coloured boxes showing cartoon characters.

If you are offering a service, rather than a product, similar principles apply. Will the service be aimed at customers who want a basic service and low prices or are you aiming to attract people who are prepared to pay more for something if they feel they are getting top-quality service? Business premises, web pages or advertisements will need to be designed accordingly to give the right image to potential customers.

A person with catering experience decides to go into business. Will it be a high street café aimed at shoppers or a more expensive restaurant serving evening meals? The design of the premises, including the interior decoration and style of furniture, will be different depending on the business.

Getting the design right is vital and can mean the difference between success and failure. Many people starting out in business feel it is worthwhile to use professional help at this stage and commission a product designer or interior decorator. The latest computer technology can also assist with design, such as Computer Aided Design (CAD) which allows a product to be viewed from all angles on a computer screen.

MARKET

The final stage is to market the goods or service. The four 'P's are often used to provide a basic starting point for new businesses.

Product

How will the product or service be promoted to potential customers? Any special or unique qualities need to be considered. At this stage, a name for the business, product or service will need to be decided on. Again, this needs to be something that will have market appeal. A further consideration might be whether a product is environmentally friendly. This could be an important selling point, for example, with a new vehicle.

Price

The price at which a product or service is sold is a crucial factor in whether it will sell. Careful thought will need to be given to the cost of production, what profit margins are expected and the price of similar products already on the market. You need to find out what your customers are prepared to pay in order to price something effectively.

Place

Place refers to where and how customers will buy a product or use a service. With many businesses, this will mean premises, such as a shop or hairdressing salon. An electrician or garden designer will carry out their business at the customer's own home. With increased use of the Internet for buying and selling, 'place' can now often mean home delivery following a purchase made online.

Promotion

Promotion is about communicating with customers so they will want to buy from you. How will this be done and what form of advertising will be used? To promote successfully, you need to know about your customers. A local fast food outlet might post an attractive menu through the letterbox of homes in the area, while a more specialist product might be advertised in a magazine or on a webpage. For example, a school uniform supplier might advertise in a school magazine. Promoting what you have to sell is crucial but careful consideration needs to be given to cost, as advertising can be very expensive.

CHECK YOUR LEARNING

1. What is an 'entrepreneur'?
2. What do you think are some of the important qualities of an entrepreneur?
3. Explain the importance of each of the following when starting a business:
   a) Research
   b) Design
   c) Market

RESEARCH AND TESTING CRUCIAL WHEN STARTING A BUSINESS

NEWS ITEM

People moving into self-employment must ensure they conduct full and proper planning before starting their company, it has been claimed.

Industry commentator Irina Patterson claimed that forming a plan, and conducting market testing, is crucial before any company commences trading. "Those who succeed put in an enormous amount of time and effort," she told Business Week. "And they look for feedback, support, and mentors who can tell them how they can improve their ideas," she stated. In contrast, those who think they can do something highly entrepreneurial very quickly inevitably fail to succeed, Ms Patterson claimed.

She added that as many as 25 per cent of entrepreneurs fail to validate their ideas before committing resources to their enterprise.

"They build products without talking to prospective customers in their target market. If you engage seriously with your customers, there's no way a business can fail," Ms Patterson said.

Too many people deciding to work for themselves are "infatuated with their own brilliance", she added, when a sensible, measured approach is the best way forward.

Source: 'Research and testing crucial when starting a new business', 25 June 2010, http://www.microsoft.com/uk/smallbusiness/sbnews/starting-up-a-small-business/Research-and-testing-crucial-when-starting-a-business-19858582.mspx
Used with permission from Microsoft.

DISCUSSION

- Why are some business ventures unsuccessful?
- What can make the difference between success and failure?

START YOUR OWN BUSINESS

You and your friends are going into business – you have had a brilliant idea!

- **Research** your idea by working through the questions what? where? who? and why?

- Produce a **design** for your goods or service and produce a poster or advertisement to promote it.

- Decide how you will **market** your product by deciding on product, price, place and promotion.

Present your idea to the rest of the class.

responsibility of being the boss can put you under immense pressure. However, the sense of achievement when you get your business up and running is unlike everything you can experience as someone else's employee. You also lose the boredom that often goes hand in hand with working for someone else. There is never a dull moment when you work for yourself. If you are independent, well prepared, un-afraid of hard work and have a high stress-tolerance then it is certainly worth thinking about opening your own business.

Source: 'Chicken Tonight?', Go for it, www.goforitni.com

CASE STUDY: ROLLO POLLO KITCHEN

Rollo Pollo is a South Belfast take-away café – with a difference! Inspired by the delicious, healthy fast food scene in Australia, Rollo Pollo offers an alternative to the high fat, additive packed world of traditional fast food. Rollo Pollo uses good, locally-sourced ingredients, free from preservatives and colourings. Combined with creative menu planning the result is fresh fast food full of flavour, but without the fat.

Rollo Pollo was established in December 2007 by Ruth Little, a former Irish athletics champion. Ruth spent time training in Sydney and after a session would pick up a healthy, low fat take-away from one of the fast food outlets close to the athletics track. On returning to Northern Ireland, Ruth decided to go into business and start her own healthy take-away food outlet. A first priority was importing a custom made chicken rotisserie from Australia. This rotisserie produces delicious, healthy chicken by draining fat from the meat while cooking but retaining the juices and flavour. As well as the Signature Rotisserie Chicken, Rollo Pollo also offers a varied menu of soups, gourmet salads, sushi and hot dishes.

Ruth says… "Opening a business is definitely not for the faint-hearted. It is a very stressful and difficult thing to undertake. There is no-one else to blame when things go wrong and the

CASE STUDY: NITRADELINKS.COM

Years of experience in the motor trade, a great idea and the support of Invest Northern Ireland's Go for it programme were the only components that Donavon McKillen needed to set up on his own in business.

The Magherafelt-born entrepreneur is the power behind nitradelinks.com, a web-based service dedicated to providing a trade-only service to motor dealers across Northern Ireland, and after only a few months is already looking to expand further.

"I had worked in the motor trade for years," said Donavon, "but I always had problems with buying and selling trade stock. Unlike other parts of Ireland or the UK, there was no service in Northern Ireland which allowed dealers to buy and sell trade vehicles online, so I decided to explore the concept. I realised that if one existed here, it would save dealers time, hassle and money by using it."

Keen to get moving on his idea, Donavon signed up for Invest NI's Go for it programme, which meant he could properly research the market and learn what he needed to do to make it a reality.

Donavon said the response to his new service has exceeded his expectations. "We have new dealers signing up every day. They are delighted by the small monthly fee charged and I'm very hopeful I can get every dealer in Northern Ireland using it eventually."

The upbeat entrepreneur puts much of his success down to what he learned through Invest NI's Go for it programme, stating, "I got to know how to assess my market properly, which involved a lot of meticulous planning and research, and it also gave me a great understanding of financial planning and all aspects of financing a business – all of which fed into the comprehensive business plan I put together while attending the Go for it programme."

"Starting my own business is the best thing I could have done," said Donavon. "I love being my own boss. Of course, I have to put a lot of hours in, but having said that, I also get flexibility when I need it."

Source: 'nitradelinks.com, Magherafelt, Co Londonderry', Go for it, www.goforitni.com

SELF-EMPLOYMENT

A person who is self-employed makes their own income by working for themselves, rather than working for someone else and being paid a wage.

Self-employment might mean a person works entirely alone, perhaps with members of the family helping out, or with a friend or business partner. Some self-employed people run their large successful business with a number of employees. When you start out in business, there are enormous opportunities, if you manage to find the product or service that people want to buy, and at the right price. The sky is the limit! On the other hand, being self-employed is usually considered to be far more risky than being employed by someone else.

THE ADVANTAGES OF SELF-EMPLOYMENT...

- **You are your own boss** – The chance to make your own decisions about your working day, rather than be told what to do, appeals to many people.

- **You work your own hours** – Of course there may be customers to consider, appointments to be kept and deadlines to meet, but self-employment gives the possibility of more flexible working hours.

- **When you work hard at something you are doing it for yourself** – Some people feel that this is a big incentive with self-employment.

- **Self-employment is a challenge** – Self-employment is hard work and certainly not an easy option, but this is what makes it attractive to some people.

- **The work is not repetitive** – In some salaried occupations, the same task is repeated over and over. With self-employment, one person may well do everything – driving, talking to customers, accounts – so the work is very varied.

- **You can be more creative and imaginative** – Some people like to try out new ideas and self-employment usually gives more scope for this.

- **No-one can make you redundant** – Self-employment is usually considered a risky option, but some people consider themselves to be more secure than if they were working for someone else.

...AND THE DISADVANTAGES

- **You may have to work long hours** – Many people who work for an employer can leave at a set time. This is not usually the case if you are self-employed. Work time may easily extend into leisure time.

- **Your income is uncertain** – With a salary you know how much to expect each month and can budget accordingly. Income from self-employment may be very erratic.

- **You do not get paid for holidays or days off** – Employees are entitled to paid leave and sick pay if they are unwell. If a self-employed person takes time off, this could mean there is no income.

- **Equipment has to be maintained** – Most businesses, however small, need some sort of equipment, transport or machinery. Having to pay for repairs or replacements could be very expensive and eat into the profits.

- **Supplies have to be bought** – With self-employment there are much greater financial outlays than with salaried employment. Essential supplies may need to be bought before the work can be carried out, and payment received.

- **You might miss the social contact** – Although being employed is not just a chance to gossip with workmates, there is an important social side of working with others. People who are self-employed may miss out on this, unless they employ other people.

- **You have to organise your own taxes and National Insurance** – Employers take care of this for their employees. Self-employed people have to sort this out for themselves, unless their business is large enough to have an accountant.

DISCUSSION

Can you think of any other advantages or disadvantages of being self-employed?

CASE STUDY: COLIN'S EXPERIENCE OF SELF-EMPLOYMENT

I'm Colin and my line of work is graphic design. Graphic design is a creative process that combines art and technology to communicate ideas. Magazines, books, and website sites are all examples of graphic design.

What are the advantages of working freelance/being self-employed?

The main advantage is that you are only answerable to yourself – you are the boss. It's also convenient (if you work from home!) and reduces transportation costs. Finally, you can make a lot of money.

What are the disadvantages?

Your income isn't guaranteed. It can be stressful and there is no official end to the working day or the working week for that matter. You also have to do your own tax and administration.

Overall, would you prefer to work for yourself or in a salaried position?

I'd prefer a salaried job, there are pros and cons for both, it just depends on the type of person you are.

What advice would you give to someone who was thinking of being self-employed?

Save some money before jumping in at the deep end – you may go a few months with no salary! Who pays the bills then! Write a Mission Statement (a short note to remind you *why* you're working for yourself). Give yourself office hours, start working and keep motivated. Only spend money on essentials items.

DISCUSSION

Organise a class debate with the motion:

"This house believes self-employment is the way out of economic recession."

Have speakers for and against the motion and elect a person to chair the debate.

CASE STUDY: DRAIN AND SEWER CONTROL

How one local man is cleaning up with dirty work.

Drain cleaning may not seem the most glamorous of careers, but for one local man it has been a platform to self-employment and, he believes, his passport to getting through the current economic downturn.

James Mallon, from Loughgall, set up his drain cleaning and sewer control company in May, following several years spent working for another drain company.

"I often thought about going out on my own," he says, "but I didn't have the confidence to do anything about it, believing that someone like me, with no experience or qualifications, could ever run their own business. Being in my 30s I also thought I was too old, that you had to be a young thing to be self-employed. But as time went on I became more and more unsettled in my job, and more and more curious about starting my own business."

Eventually James contacted the Start a Business Programme.

"The people there were so helpful," says James. "I thought they might laugh at me, but I couldn't have been more wrong. They took me and my business idea very seriously, and made me realise that age and qualifications have actually got nothing to do with a person's ability to set up their own business. It's commitment, dedication and knowledge about your business or product that counts. Well, there is nothing about drains that I don't know, and the commitment and dedication was there from the start."

James isn't worried about becoming self-employed in the current economic climate. "There will always be drains to clean," says James, "even in difficult times, and I am confident that I can provide a friendly, professional, superior and cost effective service. I really believe that if you want something, you have to go for it. I did, and going out on my own was the best move I have ever made."

Source: 'Drain Man', Go for it, www.goforitni.com

In the interview below, James comments on some of the challenges and opportunities of being self-employed …

"One of the advantages of being your own boss is that you can set your own targets and push yourself to get there. Sometimes this isn't easy! If you want to succeed in business you often have to hunt for work, as one thing is for sure, if you don't go out to attract customers you won't get them.

You meet hundreds of new people through being self-employed and make many new friends. I might get a call about a blocked sewer and the people are really in a panic to get the problem rectified. When I sort out the problem, it's not just about money, but offering the customer a service and keeping them happy. Good recommendations by word of mouth are very important to a person in business.

If I could go back and start my career all over again, I would have chosen self-employment years ago. I would advise any young person to go for self-employment if you have nothing to lose."

SELF-EMPLOYED OR UNEMPLOYED?

There are many uncertainties with self-employment, and a person may decide that it is not worth the risk of business failure and possible bankruptcy. Most people, after all, are paid by an employer rather than working for themselves. However, some people find themselves in the situation of being out of a job with no immediate prospect of finding work. Rather than face long-term unemployment, they decide to do something for themselves, and take a chance on being self-employed.

ACTIVITY

Read the case studies on pages 68–71.

- According to Ruth, Donovan, James and Colin, what are the advantages of being self-employed?
- Do they give any disadvantages?
- Do they all prefer being self-employed to working for a company?

evaluation

Assess the advantages and disadvantages of being self-employed.

SUPPORT FOR BUSINESSES IN NORTHERN IRELAND

It is not easy to turn an idea for a business into a reality. However, there are a number of agencies in Northern Ireland offering support and advice, from taking the first steps to helping a business grow and flourish.

Department for Employment and Learning (DEL)

"Our aim is to promote learning and skills to prepare people for work and to support the economy"

The Department for Employment and Learning (DEL) is one of the 11 Departments, plus the Office of the First Minister and deputy First Minister, established under the Good Friday Agreement of 1998. A member of the Local Assembly oversees the work of the Department, with the support of a Statutory Committee.

The Department's two main customer groups are:

- Individuals who are seeking to improve their levels of skills and qualifications or who require support and guidance to progress towards employment, including self-employment.
- Businesses in both the public and private sectors.

The Department has four key areas of activity:

- Enhancing the provision of learning and skills, including entrepreneurship, enterprise, management and leadership.
- Increasing the level of research and development, creativity and innovation in the Northern Ireland economy.
- Helping individuals to acquire jobs, including self-employment, and improving the linkages between employment programmes and skills development.
- The development and maintenance of the framework of employment rights and responsibilities.

Help for people looking for work

The Jobs & Benefits offices and JobCentres give advice to those who are looking for work, or people who would like to change their job. There are opportunities available for unemployed people who need training and specialist advice for people with disabilities.

The Careers Service has an interactive website that gives information about the range of careers available and helps people of all ages make informed choices. Careers Advisers are available throughout Northern Ireland to give support and guidance through face to face contact.

Help for businesses

The Employment Service, through its network of 35 Jobs & Benefits offices and JobCentres throughout Northern Ireland, offers employers a comprehensive recruitment service. This includes advertising job vacancies, providing application forms and in some instances interview facilities at no cost to the employer. These vacancies can also be viewed at jobcentreonline (www.jobcentreonline.com). Employers willing to offer employment to jobseekers who have been unemployed for 13 weeks or more may be entitled to receive an Employer Subsidy under the Steps to Work programme.

Further information on the Employer Subsidy and contact details for Jobs & Benefits offices/JobCentres can be found at www.delni.gov.uk/es/index/ publications/del-response-to-recession/recession- stw-employers-subsidy.htm

Apprenticeships

Apprenticeships have been around for many years and have proven to be an effective way for employers to train their staff. ApprenticeshipsNI is the Northern Ireland apprenticeship programme. Apprentices are employed on a permanent contract with a Northern Ireland based company to work a minimum of 21 hours; this includes the time spent on 'off-the-job' training with organisations which have

been contracted by the Department to provide training towards recognised qualifications. The employer arranges quality in-house work instruction, with the apprentice working alongside experienced staff as they learn the trade.

Apprenticeships usually take between two to four years to complete. Through an apprenticeship, employers gain staff who are skilled and qualified, helping them become more productive, effective and competitive.

Further information on ApprenticeshipsNI can be found at www.nidirect.gov.uk/apprenticeshipsNI

Steps to Work

The Department for Employment and Learning, through the Jobs & Benefits office and JobCentre network in Northern Ireland, provides a range of support and assistance for helping people into employment. Steps to Work, the Department's main adult return to work programme, is a new approach to help people find work. It offers a flexible menu of work related activities that can be adapted to suit individual needs. Some of the options include re-training, gaining qualifications, improving existing skills and work experience. Employers can take part in the scheme by offering work experience or receiving a subsidy to employ a person who has been out of work for more than 13 weeks. By supporting individuals in the community employers are helping to bring long-term benefits to the local economy.

Source: The Department for Employment and Learning, www.delni.gov.uk

Department of Enterprise, Trade and Investment (DETI)

DETI's goal is "to grow a dynamic, innovative economy"

The Department of Enterprise, Trade and Investment was established as one of the Departments under the Good Friday Agreement. DETI plays a vital role in Northern Ireland's economic development by developing policies in the areas outlined below. An example of a current priority or area of development is given next to each.

- **Enterprise** – A priority in this area is a new strategy to give better support to local enterprises. The aim is to co-ordinate the work of the various departments and organisations that have a role to play.
- **Social Economy** – The development of Social Economy has been given priority by DETI from 2008 to 2011. Social Economy is concerned with the development of the local community, particularly areas of economic disadvantage.
- **Innovation** – Stimulating business growth and encouraging new ideas are made priorities in this area.
- **Energy** – The focus for development in this area is renewable energy. DETI plans to have new regulations in place by April 2011.

- **Telecoms** – Improving broadband is a priority as high speed communications can help local businesses compete on the global market.

- **Tourism** – There is a lot of scope to boost tourism and increase the contribution it makes to the economy. DETI have made this area of development a priority.

Sponsored agencies

DETI sponsor a number of agencies that help to deliver their economic policies. These agencies are referred to as Non-Departmental Public Bodies (NDPBs).

Invest NI is responsible for business support in Northern Ireland. It is dealt with in more detail as a separate section opposite.

The Northern Ireland Tourist Board is responsible for promoting and marketing Northern Ireland as a tourist destination. NITB aims to provide excellent information and facilities to all visitors to Northern Ireland and has identified five key areas which have the best opportunities for tourism. These are Saint Patrick and the Christian Heritage; the Causeway Coast and Glens of Antrim; the Mournes; the Walled City of Derry; and the *Titanic*.

The Health and Safety Executive for Northern Ireland is responsible for promoting and enforcing health and safety at work. It aims to reduce work-related injuries and ill-health. HSENI does this by providing information for the workplace and carrying out regular inspections to make sure that the regulations are being followed.

The Consumer Council for Northern Ireland

is responsible for protecting and promoting the interests of consumers in Northern Ireland. The Consumer Council deals with transport, fuel, water, money affairs, education and business. It gives information to people about these services and makes sure that consumer issues are taken into account when new policies are made.

DETI has the overall responsibility for supporting businesses and protecting consumers in Northern Ireland.

For further information visit: www.detini.gov.uk

Source: © Crown copyright, public sector information licensed under the Open Government Licence v1.0.

Invest Northern Ireland

"Building locally competing globally"

Invest NI aims to encourage growth in the local economy. It does this by:

- Helping new and existing businesses to compete internationally.
- Attracting new investments into Northern Ireland.

Invest NI is part of the Department of Enterprise, Trade and Investment (DETI) and provides strong government support for local businesses. Invest NI offers a range of programmes, services and expert advice for businesses in Northern Ireland.

Start a business

Thousands of new businesses start in Northern Ireland each year. Invest NI can help by offering a range of programmes and all the guidance and support needed to help turn business dreams into a reality! Starting a business needs a lot of preparation – marketing plans, finding premises and getting the necessary funding. Invest NI can help with all of these and increase the chance of the business being a success.

Grow your business

Whether to grow or stay the same is a situation every business has to face. Invest NI have programmes and services to help businesses face the challenge of being more efficient, more competitive and able to achieve growth in the global market place.

Locate in Northern Ireland

Companies from overseas that locate their business in Northern Ireland also give the economy a boost, and the local job market. Invest NI actively promotes Northern Ireland to investors from abroad, by pointing out the many advantages of locating here. These include:

- Excellent communication and transport networks.
- A highly educated, English-speaking workforce.
- Competitive costs.
- Financial incentives and on-going support.
- Northern Ireland is a great place to live!

Invest NI supports businesses as they start up, grow and develop and then move into the global market. By encouraging foreign trade and investments, the local economy is made stronger, employment prospects improve and the whole community can benefit.

For further information visit www.investni.com/index.htm

CASE STUDY: ALLEN AND OVERY LOCATE IN NORTHERN IRELAND

The international Law firm, Allen and Overy, has recently set up an office in Belfast creating over 300 high quality jobs. The investment is being supported by Invest Northern Ireland, which has offered assistance of £2.5 million.

Allen and Overy is one of the world's largest international law firms, with 36 offices in 26 countries and over 5,000 staff. The Belfast office will be home to a new Support and Legal Services Centre, which will deliver a range of support functions such as IT, HR and financial management, as well as transaction support to its legal teams servicing Allen and Overy clients based outside Northern Ireland.
Announcing the investment Enterprise Minister Arlene Foster said:

"This investment, which will create over 300 quality jobs including up to 60 legal posts, is a tremendous endorsement of the Northern Ireland proposition. It reflects the confidence that international firms have in what we can offer, in particular our highly skilled and loyal workforce, low cost working environment and technically advanced infrastructure.

Allen and Overy evaluated 20 locations worldwide before deciding on Northern Ireland and was strongly influenced by the support offered by Invest NI and by our universities and representatives of the legal fraternity who championed our talented people. I hope that this investment will act as a catalyst for future investment in the legal services sector here which is recognised as an important sector in promoting economic growth."

Source: http://www.investni.com/about-news. htm?newsid=15564

CASE STUDY: BUBBLE LANDS SUCCESS IN SAUDI MARKETPLACE

Digital technology specialist Bubble (NI) has won its first business in Saudi Arabia from its participation in an Invest Northern Ireland trade mission to the important Gulf marketplace. The Belfast-based company is to provide a series of Arab and English language video presentations on health and safety issues to United Arab Can Manufacturing Company (UAC) in Damman, a business producing 1.4 billion cans a year for international clients to customers throughout the Middle East.

The videos will be based on the company's successful and highly adaptable 'Speechbubble' software platform.

The animated videos are being developed by Bubble and will run in a continuous loop on screens across the huge factory to highlight health and safety procedures.

Dr Vicky Kell, Invest NI Trade Director, welcoming Bubble's latest success in Gulf markets, said: "Bubble (NI) is now beginning to reap the business rewards of a determined approach to the Gulf, especially Saudi Arabia which continues to be among the most dynamic global economies."

Source: http://www.investni.com/about-news. htm?newsid=14499

KEY QUESTION

What has attracted Allen and Overy to Northern Ireland?

KEY QUESTION

What has helped Bubble to achieve success outside Northern Ireland?

- Use the Internet to find other examples of Invest NI's success stories.
- Give examples of the different ways that Invest NI supports business.

Enterprise Northern Ireland

"Representing the Local Enterprise Agency network"

Local Enterprise Agencies are independent, non-profit making companies set up to support small businesses and help to develop the local economy. Enterprise Northern Ireland (ENI) is the organisation which represents this network of local groups across Northern Ireland. ENI's vision is to contribute to the development of the Northern Ireland economy by supporting entrepreneurship and business enterprise.

One of the most important areas of ENI's work is to provide suitable premises for new businesses at an affordable cost. LEAs currently provide a base for over 2,000 businesses across Northern Ireland. ENI also run a range of programmes to help entrepreneurs get on the right path with setting up their business and help it stay on course.

Need help with a business idea?

Pre-Start Programmes help to develop a business idea. The Exploring Enterprise Programme focuses on the needs of people who have recently lost their job or been out of work for some time. It concentrates on rebuilding confidence and encouraging people to try and achieve their personal career ambitions.

Want to start a business?

Start-Up Programmes help a business to get going and cope with the first few months of trading. The Go for it programme can help with ideas and planning and is designed to help potential entrepreneurs launch their own business. The programme includes a personal business advisor, training plan and one-to-one advice. There are special initiatives for female entrepreneurs, minority communities and community enterprise.

Want to improve your business?

Once a business is established, Business Improvement Programmes will help it develop and grow. Tradelinks is a micro-enterprise development programme managed and delivered jointly by ENI and the Enterprise Boards in the six border counties of the Republic of Ireland. Through Tradelinks, micro-enterprises will become more sustainable and competitive, thereby generating greater added value, earnings and wealth in their host communities. Tradelinks' objectives are to build export capability, encourage new market and new product development.

Enterprise Northern Ireland plays an important role in supporting the local economy. ENI represents the interests of Local Enterprise Agencies and co-ordinates a range of programmes to help develop a business from the first ideas through to global trading.

Source: www.enterpriseni.com
For further information visit the Enterprise Northern Ireland website.

The Prince's Trust

"The Prince's Trust helps change young lives"

In the UK, around one in five young people are not in work, education or training. The Prince's Trust gives practical and financial support to the young people who need it most. They help to develop key skills, confidence and motivation so young people can gain qualifications, find employment, set up a community project or even start their own business.

The Prince's Trust have four key target groups:

- Unemployed young people
- Young people underachieving in education
- Young people leaving care
- Young offenders and ex-offenders

The information that follows is taken from The Prince's Trust website: www.princes-trust.org.uk

Programmes to support young people

The Prince's Trust run programmes that encourage young people to take responsibility for themselves – helping them build the life they choose rather than the one they've ended up with. More than three in four young people on Prince's Trust schemes move into work, education or training:

- **The Enterprise Programme** provides money and support to help young people start up in business. The Prince's Trust has helped more than 77,000 young people to set up their own businesses since 1983.
- **The Team Programme** is a 12 week personal development course, offering work experience, qualifications, practical skills, community projects and a residential week.
- **Get intos** are short courses offering intensive training and experience in a specific sector to help young people get a job.

- **Development Awards** are small grants to enable young people to access education, training or work.
- **Community Cash Awards** are grants to help young people set up a project that will benefit their community.
- **xl clubs** give young people who are at risk of truanting, exclusion and underachievement the chance to turn their lives around.

The Prince's Trust Celebrate Success awards

Every year, The Prince's Trust honours young people who have overcome barriers including long-term unemployment, homelessness and depression to turn their lives around at the Celebrate Success awards.

You can read the stories of these young people on The Prince's Trust website: www.princes-trust.org.uk/celebratesuccess

RESEARCH ACTIVITY

Use the Internet to research sources of finance that might be available to an entrepreneur.

WHO CAN HELP?

Five different organisations have been described, all offering support for businesses in Northern Ireland. Which one do you think would be the best to offer advice in each of the following situations?

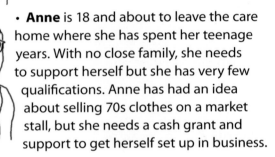

- **Trevor** is middle-aged. He has been unemployed for six months following redundancies at the factory where he worked. There are very few job opportunities in his former line of work, so he is thinking about getting some careers advice on re-training.

- **Anne** is 18 and about to leave the care home where she has spent her teenage years. With no close family, she needs to support herself but she has very few qualifications. Anne has had an idea about selling 70s clothes on a market stall, but she needs a cash grant and support to get herself set up in business.

- **Freda** makes home-made tray bakes and fruit pies which are very popular with local shops. She wants to expand her business and supply supermarkets and the catering industry. Who could give her the advice she needs?

- **George** is Managing Director of Home Electrics, a national company producing electrical appliances. They are thinking of locating one of their factories, and possibly their headquarters, in Northern Ireland. Who could give the best advice on whether this is the right move for the business?

1. What are the risks involved with setting up your own business?

2. How does the Department for Employment and Learning (DEL) help individuals to find work?

3. In what ways does DEL help employers?

4. One of DETI's activities is to boost tourism in Northern Ireland. What are the benefits of doing this?

5. What help does Enterprise Northern Ireland offer to local businesses?

6. Give examples of how The Prince's Trust offers support to young people.

EXAM FOCUS

Each chapter has focussed on exam skills. Examiners refer to these skills as Assessment Objectives. So far, we have covered:

AO1 – demonstrating your knowledge and understanding
AO2 – applying your knowledge and understanding

The final skill to practice is:

AO3 – Showing the ability to investigate, analyse and evaluate information.

Questions testing AO3 usually require a longer answer. To gain high marks you will need to write clearly, organise your material and develop your ideas. Your answer will be based partly on your own knowledge and partly on a short article you will be given to read.

The following question tests this skill:

With reference to the extract below and your own knowledge assess the advantages and disadvantages to an entrepreneur of locating a business in Northern Ireland.

[10 marks]

"Northern Ireland is a perfect place for the location of a new business. Over 700 foreign investors and many from the United Kingdom have decided to move here. Northern Ireland has great expertise in hi-tech skills, industrial creativity and a great lifestyle to offer."

TIME

1 hour 30 m

INSTRUCT

Write your C
Answer **all si**

INFORMATI

The total mark
Quality of writ
Figures in brac
question or part

ADVICE TO CA

You are advised t
examination time

each

EXAM FOCUS...

"Northern Ireland's attractive business appeal is based on:

- *fresh talent pool on one of the youngest populations in the European Union.*
- *a highly educated, English speaking workforce.*
- *excellent transport and communications links.*
- *great recreational facilities.*
- *many incentives and support from Invest NI (Invest Northern Ireland).*
- *a good value for money environment."*

Extract © CCEA from GCSE Learning for Life and Work Modular Specimen Assessment Materials, Unit 5: Employability Specimen Paper, Subject Code 4810
Insert 1: Employability, Source C, entitled, 'Why should a business locate in Northern Ireland?', page 34

The extract will help you to write about the advantages for an entrepreneur locating in Northern Ireland. For this type of question, it is important not to write a one-sided answer, and you also need to consider disadvantages as well.

You might wish to consider the following points:

- Locating overseas may involve lower taxes.
- Higher wages may need to be paid in Northern Ireland.
- Production costs and raw materials may be cheaper overseas.

TIM

1 hou

INS

Wri
Ans

IN

Th
Q
F
q

...ded.

...ks awarded to each

...ting the available

GLOSSARY

ASSISTIVE TECHNOLOGY: This is new computer technology that is being developed for the workplace to help employees who are disabled.

BUSINESS ETHICS: This involves businesses acting in a responsible way towards employees, the community and the environment.

CAREER PLAN: A career plan is a road map that helps a person reach their destination in the world of work.

CONTRACT OF EMPLOYMENT: A contract of employment is an agreement between the employer and employee. This contract is made as soon as a person accepts a job and an employee is entitled to a written contract within two months of starting work.

CURRICULUM VITAE: A Curriculum Vitae (CV) is a summary of a person's education and employment history, giving details of qualifications, training and experience.

DISCRIMINATION: This means to be treated in a less favourable way than other people. It includes the workplace, at school or having access to important services, such as healthcare.

ECONOMY: The economy of a particular country, or area, is concerned with the production of goods and services and how they are distributed and consumed.

E-MARKETING: This refers to the promotion of products or services using the Internet.

EMIGRATION: This is the act of leaving a country permanently to live elsewhere.

EMPLOYABILITY: This term means that a person is capable of finding work in the first place, making a success of their job and being able to change careers successfully if needed.

ENTREPRENEUR: This term refers to a business person who is able to spot an opportunity and market it successfully, taking calculated risks along the way.

EQUALITY: Equality means equal rights for people regardless of how they might be different to someone else. Equality can involve both equal treatment and equal opportunity.

EXPORTS: A country's exports are the goods and produce which are sold abroad.

GLOBALISATION: This is the process of the world becoming more interconnected and interdependent, particularly in regard to trade and business.

HOT DESKING: This term refers to a working situation where a desk, computer and workspace are available to anyone who needs them in the organisation, on a flexible basis.

IMMIGRATION: This is when new citizens come into a particular area, to settle permanently.

IMPORTS: These are the products, services or raw materials which are brought into a country.

LIFELONG LEARNING: This term refers to the idea that once someone is in employment, the learning process will continue and will also involve professional development and acquiring new work-related skills.

MIGRATION: This means a move from one place to another, usually looking for more favourable conditions. Sometimes people migrate when looking for work, as seasonal opportunities become available.

SOCIAL RESPONSIBILITY: This means a business makes decisions not just aimed at profit, but also considering what is best for the community and the environment, both locally and globally.

SOFT SKILLS: This term refers to personal qualities such as team work, initiative and communication. They are becoming increasingly important, along with education and experience.

SUSTAINABILITY: A sustainable business does not have a negative impact on the environment; the methods used in production and the end product will be environmentally friendly and renewable where possible.

TELEWORKING: This refers to work that needs a telephone, computer and perhaps a fax machine. As many people have these items in their house, their work can be carried out at home most of the time with no need to travel to the workplace.

TOWN TWINNING: This is the idea of pairing cities across the world as a way of making links between nations. This pairing can lead to cultural links, economic trade and student exchanges.

TRADE UNION: A Trade Union represents the rights of employees in the workplace, ensuring that employers meet their legal obligations and responsibilities. These might include working hours, pay or health and safety issues.

INDEX

COPYRIGHT INFORMATION

Copyright has been acknowledged to the best of our ability. If there are any inadvertent errors or omissions, we shall be happy to correct them in any future editions.

Acknowledgements

Questions from the following papers are included with the permission of the Northern Ireland Council for the Curriculum, Examinations and Assessment:

CCEA's GCSE Learning for Life and Work Modular Paper, Unit 5: Employability, May 2010, GLW61; GCSE Learning for Life and Work Modular Specimen Assessment Materials, Unit 5: Employability Specimen Paper, Subject Code 4810. © CCEA

Thanks to the following organisations and copyright holders for their kind permission to use their logos, titles, images and information:

About Equal Opportunities; Bryson Recycling; Chain Reaction Cycles; Department for Employment and Learning (DEL); Department of Enterprise, Trade and Investment (DETI); Directgov; Drain & Sewer Control; Enterprise Northern Ireland (ENI); Equality Commission for Northern Ireland; Invest Northern Ireland; McDonalds; McGees Butchers; Microsoft; Net Regs; nitradelinks.com; Norbrook Laboratories Ltd; Retail Systems Technology (RST EPOS); Rollo Pollo; SMV Textiles Group; South Tyrone Empowerment Programme (STEP); The Prince's Trust; The Well-Being Hub

The image on page 42 is from the Library of Congress, Prints and Photographs Division, National Child Labour Committee Collection, reproduction number LC-DIG-nclc-05394. According to the library there are no restrictions of any kind on the use of the Hine photographic material. Information on this is available at http://www.loc.gov/rr/print/res/097_hine.html

Picture credits

All photographs are by iStock Photo except for the following which are included with kind permission of the copyright holders. The numbers denote page numbers.

Cezary Piwowarski: 56
Drain & Sewer Control: 71
Invest Northern Ireland: 68
Jule Berlin: 74 (right)
Library of Congress, Prints and Photographs Division: 42
P177: 12

ALSO IN THIS SERIES

Presented in the same clear and visually stimulating format as *Learning for Life and Work: EMPLOYABILITY*, these resources include activities, questions, discussion starters, news items, information files and case studies to encourage active engagement with the topics.

Learning for Life and Work:
PERSONAL DEVELOPMENT
ISBN: 978-1-906578-56-5

This book follows the specification for unit 3.2, enabling pupils to develop a deeper understanding of their own personal development and learn how to manage the challenges that they may face through life.

Learning for Life and Work:
LOCAL AND GLOBAL CITIZENSHIP
ISBN: 978-1-906578-71-8

This book follows the specification for unit 3.1, making complex issues accessible and encouraging students to understand their own role as contributors to society.

Contact Colourpoint Educational at:

Tel: 9182 6339   **Fax:** 9182 1900
Email: sales@colourpoint.co.uk
Web: www.colourpoint.co.uk

Colourpoint Books, Colourpoint House, Jubilee Business Park, Jubilee Road, Newtownards, Co Down, BT23 4YH

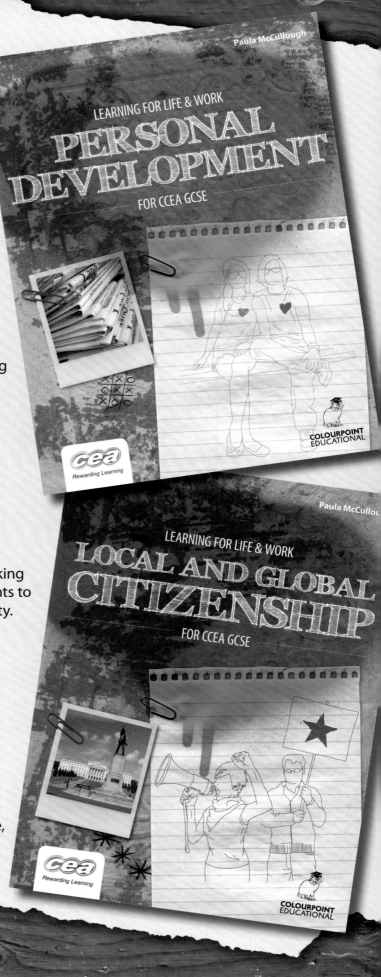